Some of us are Black

by Charles Walker

Foreword by Lord Scarman

SOME OF US ARE BLACK
by Charles Walker

© Family Publications, 1993

ISBN 1 871217 12 1

published by
FAMILY PUBLICATIONS
Wicken, Milton Keynes, MK19 6BU, UK
Telephone: **0908 57234** *Fax:* **0908 57331**

cover design by
Joanna Pitt

printed in England by
BPCC Wheatons Ltd
Marsh Barton, Exeter, EX2 8RP

Charles Walker was born in South London in 1924, educated at St Olave's Grammar School; Queens' College, Cambridge; and at Wells Theological College. He became an Anglican priest in 1950 and was curate at St Mary's, Woolwich and afterwards chaplain at Peterhouse, Cambridge.

He entered the Catholic Church in 1961 and after four years at the Beda College in Rome, he was ordained a Catholic priest in 1966. He became particularly interested in the Black Community while serving in the parish of Corpus Christi, Brixton Hill. In 1973 he was appointed its Chaplain. He was also National Chaplain of the Young Christian Workers Movement from 1973 to 1980. He was made a Chapter Canon of Southwark in 1982.

The author at a multi-cultural Mass with Alphonso Maquis and Agatha Deniel, members of the South London Catholic Caribbean Community.

Contents

Foreword by Lord Scarman

I had the good fortune to see at first hand some of Charles Walker's fine work in South London. Now in this book he tells the story. As the story unfolds, the reader will be carried forward by the joy and enthusiasm which he kindled amongst those with whom and for whom he worked. It is an exciting story: he has had his failures, which he describes with candour: he has had his successes, which he is careful never to exaggerate. He fell in love with the Caribbean people, their charm, their laughter, their art, their wonderful sense of family, and their gift of personal friendship and loyalty. If you are not already proud and delighted that so many Caribbean people have made Britain their home, I guarantee you will be persuaded well before you finish this entrancing look at their struggle to win justice, equal opportunities, and freedom from the pernicious evils of racial prejudice and discrimination.

In a very real sense Canon Walker was chaplain to the Caribbean community in South London. He is, of course, a Catholic: but the clergy of South London worked, and to-day continue to work, together while maintaining their own denominations. Indeed, the work of the churches in South London has not won the recognition they deserve. And the churches have learned much from their Caribbean church-goers. I have no doubt that there is much more joyous music and singing to be heard in church today in Brixton, Wandsworth and Clapham than there was before the Caribbean people arrived.

Not the least of Canon Walker's achievements was his tremendous success as first chairman of the Consultative Group established after the Brixton disorders of 1981. He begins the story on page 91. This is perhaps the most important chapter in the book. There have been those who have doubted whether direct consultation between police and people could be made to produce useful results. Charles Walker was instrumental in making consultation in Brixton a real success. And if so in Brixton, why not also elsewhere? This chapter should be studied by all who care for good relations between police and the community they police.

It is no surprise to me that Charles Walker's account of his chaplaincy in South London is entertaining, instructive and lively. But it is more: it is a historical document with a message for us all. A plural society need not be confined to racial tensions and jealousies: it can be a culturally rich, exciting and friendly world.

Preface

"Some of us are black" is a story of discovery and education. At Brixton in the late sixties, I discovered Britain's Black Community. During the four years I served in the parish of Corpus Christi, Brixton Hill, I gradually learned to value the rich humanity of our people from the Caribbean. And because they were in some degree "sheep without a shepherd", I was willing to be their man. Perhaps it would have been better if there were priests of Caribbean origin to serve them, as the Irish community had been served by Irish priests when they began to come to Britain in large numbers. However, black priests from the Caribbean seemed not to be available, at least in those days. It was then incumbent on the native clergy of England to learn how to look after our black people with some degree of effectiveness. So in offering myself as a priest for our Caribbean people, I knew I was embarking on a very large learning process.

The story that follows tells first of my initiation at Brixton and then twenty years of learning as Caribbean Chaplain in South London. I have come to understand a good deal about our people, sometimes by making mistakes. But I know that there are areas of black consciousness that I will never be able to share. The people understand this when, with some of them, I struggle to comprehend a little patois - they laugh with me and accommodate their thoughts into English for my benefit. There is, however, an advantage in being a white priest in a black community. Their home now is Britain and they need bridges into the predominantly white set-up - both for Church and secular purposes. I have tried to be useful to our people in this respect too.

I have called the story "Some of us are black". I hope these words make the point that we all belong together in modern Britain. The key word in the title is the "us". We can think negatively about Multi-Racial Britain and growl that we are "stuck with one another" through the complex inter-play of our country's colonial history and people's quest for a better life. But with a little imagination and generosity of spirit we can do better than that: we can see the influx of Caribbean and other "new Britons" as a marvellous enrichment of our Church and our Society.

Brixton in the sixties

I arrived at the Roman Catholic parish of Corpus Christi, Brixton Hill in South London, on July 26th, 1966 the Saturday afternoon that England beat West Germany in the World Cup. I took this as a good augury. A two-line letter from the Vicar General of Southwark Diocese, the Archbishop's second-in-command, had directed me there. This was after four years of preparation for the Catholic priesthood in Rome. I was 42 years old and the new curate. I was a late starter because I had previously been an Anglican priest for ten years.

I am a South Londoner by birth and up-bringing so I was coming to a reasonably familiar scene. In the sixties, mention of Brixton immediately rang up two images - the prison and black people. The latter image was verified at once as I arrived. Every third face on Brixton Hill, or so it seemed, was a black one. I thought of myself as a man of good will in racial matters - was it not my job to be! - but that apart, I was almost totally ignorant of black people.

Irish induction

At Corpus Christi, I quickly discovered that I was in the bosom of the Irish. The parish priest was a Kerry man and my fellow curate (shortly to be replaced) was from Waterford. We had two sisters (family sisters) looking after the parish house who hailed from Tipperary. In the late sixties, Catholic congregations were very large with very many habitual attenders.

Sixteen hundred or more crowded into the Church every Sunday for the five masses, including the Saturday evening one. A large proportion of these were Irish born people or people of Irish ancestry. In addition to the masses at the

1

parish Church, we had two "out-stations" - the Allardyce Hall at the far end of the parish and a community centre on the Tulse Hill Estate - and Brixton Prison. The prison had a mass and an afternoon service and there were always baptisms in the Church in the afternoons. Sundays at Corpus Christi were quite strenuous.

Despite the large numbers of black people in the neighbourhood, only a sprinkling of them appeared in the Church. The easy assumption was that very few of them were Catholics. This proved not to be the case. Then as now, at least fifteen per cent of our Caribbean people were Catholics and they came from very vibrant Catholic cultures back home. Their absence from Church became a very important pastoral problem.

But there was no doubt that the culture of Corpus Christi was Anglo-Irish with the accent heavily on the Irish. English though I was, the people gave me an immediate welcome. I was short of my right arm, having lost it as a child in a street accident. Everyone was vastly intrigued to know how I was going to manage at Mass, especially at giving out Holy Communion. I could feel a round of silent applause as I hung my little specially adapted ciborium round my neck on the first Sunday morning. On this score, the parish priest had already been marvellously sensitive. The sacristy at the Church had accommodated a large statue of the Sacred Heart which had one of its hands broken off. Years afterwards, I came across this statue in the home of one of our parishioners. At the request of the parish priest, the lady of the house had agreed to hide it in her home to avoid any risk of hurting my feelings.

At Brixton I became an honorary Irishman. It was soon true that nearly all things Irish delighted me. The wit was constant, so was the humanity. We had a large number of splendid families. And Irish people generally love the Church and would do anything for it. Being a priest among the Irish is very ego-boosting. You can easily begin to believe that you are at least as infallible as the Pope. I did, however, come across a few embittered Irish folk and I began to learn that there is a dark side to the moon in Ireland.

During these days, Irish lads and girls were coming over to England in a continuous stream. I became good friends with several large collections of brothers and sisters and in one I held the franchise for the family weddings. I officiated for four of the brothers and sisters before I left Brixton. It was during the reception at one of these weddings that I was introduced to "poteen". The father of the groom poured me out half a tumbler full of white liquid from a secret supply he had brought with him from Ireland. One sip nearly blew my head off.

I took to going on holiday in Ireland and for a succession of summers found my way to a different magical spot on the west coast. From County Cork to Donegal the coast line is breath-takingly beautiful. I used to pitch my little tent anywhere that took my fancy - only occasionally was it appropriate to ask for permission - and commune with the soul of Ireland. Each spot I chose seemed to be more ravishing than the last. But the weather is very variable in the West of Ireland. I spent many hours peering into mist and rain.

I always had families of Brixton parishioners to visit when I was over there. Bacon and cabbage came my way for the first time on one of these visits. On another, I was taken in search for Irish ragwort which flowers exclusively on Ben Bulben, a mountain which broods over Sligo Bay. With these connections and being a priest I had a better chance of feeling the heartbeat of Ireland than is possible for most English visitors.

I became a student of Irish history and of Anglo-Irish affairs. The current troubles in the North of Ireland began during my days at Corpus Christi. One of our girls was a student at Coleraine and took part in the early civil rights marches. As the situation deteriorated, we had republican collectors outside the Church on Sunday mornings despite the parish priest's discouragement.

Outreach to the black community

This story, however, is really about Brixton and the black community. There was a good deal of inter-connection between black and Irish people in Brixton in the sixties. Many of them shared the same poverty and also, the outreach of the parish towards the Caribbean community was made to a very large extent by young Irish men and women.

My visiting area of the parish was the Railton Road district, the area most populous with black people. As a result of the riots of 1981 and 1985, Railton Road began to be as internationally well-known as the Falls Road in Belfast but at this time it was fairly peaceable. It was already a district with multiple distresses. Nearly all the houses were in multiple occupation. Somerleyton Road was the horror story of those days. The houses were all four-storied with basements. I estimated that forty souls lived in one of them. There was a cooker on the landing of nearly every floor with a heap of household paraphernalia around it. These landings and the staircases were usually in a dreadful state. I remember trying to talk with a black lady on one of these landings as she washed some plates in half a bowlful of dirty water with two wide-eyed children at her skirts. And these were not the worst days. Previously, some of the basements had been drinking dives; Lambeth Council had at least succeeded in closing these down and bricking up the windows and doors.

I visited a Caribbean couple at the top of a Somerleyton house one evening. I climbed up the staircase strewn with the usual debris and dirt and knocked at the flat door. It was opened for me by a smiling face and I stepped inside to a little three-roomed palace. The brightness of their home, its cosiness and good order were an amazing contrast to the staircase approach and the dreary street outside.

4

From these visits and other encounters, I gradually learned more about Caribbean and also about African people. The civil war in Nigeria was raging when, in the course of a single evening, I called on one couple who were Ibos from the Eastern region and another who were Hausas from the North. I had a rapid induction into the tribal complexities of the African continent. On another occasion, I heard all about St Lucia for the first time. It was an easy supposition that Jamaica was synonymous with the West Indies. Virtually all the people from the small island of St Lucia were Catholics, I learned, and this was also true of the Dominicans. Years later, I made several trips to the West Indies and discovered a lot more. The religious allegiance of the people depended greatly on their colonial past. If an island or territory had been British since the seventeenth century as effectively Jamaica, Barbados, Antigua, St Vincent and St Kitts had been, then the proportion of Catholics was roughly the same as in Britain. If the Spaniards or French had held a place for a significant length of time then the predominating religion would be Catholic and the culture would be Catholic. In St Lucia and Dominica, French priests under a benign British administration, had made ninety per cent of the people Catholic. There were high proportions of Catholics in the other islands of the Eastern Caribbean. These proportions and the influx into Britain of people from the whole of the Caribbean added up to the fact that at least fifteen per cent of our total West Indian population were Catholics.

To begin with, however, I shared the lamentable ignorance of most parish clergy about West Indians. The people must have realised this and felt greatly discouraged. If the ignorance bordered on unfriendliness and sometimes went beyond that into rejection, this was enough to discourage all but the most fervent Catholics. Many West Indian Catholics have rejection stories to tell from their early days in Britain. Sometimes the rebuffs were not meant, they were a facet of the ignorance or shyness of the natives. But not all the hurts can be explained in this way. When the Irish began to come

5

to Britain in large numbers, they brought their priests with them. These priests were generally their only champions in a hostile society. Our Caribbean and African people had no such champions and interpreters except a few of their own people already established here and employed as welfare officers by the government. One such was Sir Leary Constantine, the former West Indian cricketer, but he and a few others like him were very thinly spread.

The learning process

It was not too difficult after a while to appreciate why so few Caribbean Catholics were coming to Church. Apart from feeling ill-understood and sometimes unwelcome, at least as powerful an inhibiting factor was sheer exhaustion. Sunday needed to be a day of rest and for the women a chance to catch up with the house-work. Many black women had two jobs and one at least would be at unsocial hours. We had men in Brixton whose working days began in the early hours when groups of them piled into the car of one of them and they set out for an hour and a half's journey for an early shift at the Ford works at Dagenham or the aircraft factory at Weybridge.

There were also very few black children in our Catholic day school. Corpus Christi had a big primary school of around 400 children. In the times we are speaking of, only about ten of these were black children. The county primary school three streets away soon had between a quarter and a third of its children from the black community. The dearth of black children in Catholic schools was partly explained by ordinary human dynamics. These were the days of huge over-subscription. We could easily have filled Corpus Christi primary school twice over. The white families knew this and put the new baby's name down shortly after birth. With one child from a family at the school, it was very difficult to turn down the subsequent ones. The black families generally left their application until the child was nearly old enough to start school. There were also questions about whether the parents came to Mass. By stages, black parents ceased to expect to get their children into the parish school. And once the eldest child had gone to a county school, it was certain that the younger brothers and sisters would follow.

I never knew of any disposition, still less a policy, of excluding black children, but it was a case of what later came to be called "unconscious racism" - the very circumstances discriminated against black people without any explicitly hostile intent. The situation called for a little "positive discrimination" - this phrase too became part of the glossary of race relations. The head teacher would tell me when she had a vacancy in a particular class and I would leg it round to one of our black families and urge them to claim the place. The short-comings of the admissions policy of Catholic schools was eventually exposed by a study published under the auspices of the recently formed Catholic Commission for Racial Justice called "Where Creed and Colour Matter". This was one of the early achievements of the Commission which went on to produce a long list of valuable studies, many of which brought attitudes and practices within the Catholic community under criticism.

The schools admissions problem gradually came right, partly as a result of increased awareness and deliberate action and partly, during the late seventies and eighties, of the fall in the overall school population. Now all the Catholic schools, primary and secondary, in inner-city areas are multi-racial and fairly reflect the human make-up of their Catholic communities. Indeed, in some places Catholic schools are under pressure to take Moslem and other non-christian pupils and in at least one case a Catholic school has a majority of non-christian Asian children. It remains a Catholic school in ethos and teaching with the agreement of the Asian parents; at the same time, careful respect is shown to the religion and culture of the Asian children.

At Corpus Christi, with a gallon of children to a pint pot of a school, we had to lay on basic Catholic education for all our boys and girls who went to county schools and would otherwise miss the necessary preparation for First Holy Communion and Confirmation. I was the impresario of this undertaking and it was a very large one. We had at least two hundred children on the books and well over a one hundred attendances each week - more as the big events approached. Saturday mornings were the gathering time. Our catechetical team consisted of three Notre-Dame sisters, several volunteer teachers, active and retired, a number of enthusiastic but untrained young people, some of them members of the Legion of Mary. We had groups of children in all the classrooms of the day school. After classes, all the children were shepherded into the Church for prayers and occasionally for the service of Benediction. Both teachers and children became quite a little community of interest. We had outings, parties and entertainments. By means of the Saturday morning classes a large number of boys and girls received what were then both sacraments received in the years of childhood. At the annual celebration of First Holy Communion and when the Archbishop came for Confirmation, the "catechism children" would out-number the day school children by two to one.

I once tallied up the ethnic origin of our catechism children and found that there were at least twenty different homelands represented. Italy, Spain, Portugal, even France, were on the list. We had a child or two from Libya. But over half the total were Afro-Caribbean - proof enough (if any was needed) that large numbers of our black people were Catholics.

Young people lead the way

The Irish curate whose place I took and also another Irish curate whom I joined had built up the Legion of Mary remarkably. No other parish in South London had as many young activists as we had. The Legion is an organisation of missionary minded Catholics who work with great discipline

8

and generosity under the direction of the priests. It is pre-Second Vatican Council in outlook and its spirituality - as its name declares - is very much focused on the Virgin Mary. At Corpus Christi, we had around sixty young people - mostly of Irish origin - committed to the Legion. I was "spiritual director" at various times to three groups of legionaries: one was a group of juniors of primary school age who used to visit sick and housebound folk and do shopping and housework for them. Another was a teenage group which concerned itself heavily with young people's problems, including the incipient drug allurement. A third was a group of young adults which accepted a special responsibility for reaching out to the black community.

Permission to celebrate Mass in private houses had recently come through from Rome. Our older Legion groups with their priest spiritual directors decided to organise a series of house masses in some of our woebegone streets and blocks of flats. We would choose a family who were practising the Faith and ask them to invite in some of their neighbours and friends. These did not all have to be Catholics. We had some remarkable evenings. Often the living room would be crowded with people of all ages; some would not have been to Mass for many years, for others it would be the first time they had ever experienced a Catholic Mass, let alone a Mass in somebody's home. The Mass had only recently ceased to be in Latin and some of the Caribbean participants who remembered only the Latin Mass in their homelands were inclined to think that the Mass in English was another white man's trick. But nearly always we had a splendid enthusiastic celebration. And we always sang. This at least made it more like home. For black Catholics, this was one of the mystifying characteristics of Church-going in England, "the people don't sing - how can you worship the Lord without singing!". When I visited the West Indies for the first time in the mid-seventies, I was to realise what an enormous contrast there was between the warmth and exuberance of Catholic worship in the Caribbean compared with the Sunday staple in

9

England in the sixties. We gradually got better as the liturgical changes of the Second Vatican Council came into effect. Even so, as I discovered later, Caribbean song and a vibrant sense of the power of God's word could be a marvellous enhancement to worship in England, an enhancement which is as welcome to white worshippers as black.

Another important development led by the young people of the parish was the launching of the youth clubs. There were several strands in this development. I had arrived in Brixton with a firm desire to start a section of the Young Christian Workers Movement (YCW). I had learned about it in Rome. My grip on the leading ideas of the YCW was imperfect but I had got the sense of an organisation which could motivate and educate ordinary working youth. At Corpus Christi, however, I found a very impressive network of Legion of Mary groups which were engaging in activities which are normally more in the line of the YCW.

The specific difference between the Legion and the YCW can be described in this way: the Legion exists to help the priest to do his apostolic work; in the YCW, the role of the priest is to help young people to do theirs. So Legion members do a lot of parish visiting; they compile parish censuses, engage in catechises and what was often referred to as "convert work". It is a very Church orientated organisation. In contrast, the YCW tells its youngsters to "start with life". They are shown how to notice important things that happen to them from day to day, how to reflect on their human and Christian significance, and how to take sensible action to right wrongs. So most of the YCW's preoccupations are not within the Church community but in the world outside.

Despite the excellent Legion network that we had and despite the effective work it was doing in broader terms than Church work alone, I did go ahead and start the YCW. After a false start, I managed to get a promising group together and its first major commitment was to organise a public meeting on "The needs of Young People in Brixton". The chief borough youth officer came, representatives of existing youth clubs, a good number of Legion members, and also the manager of the Ram Jam - at that time a thriving disco-hall catering mainly for black young people. As a result, we launched what was meant to be a mixed race youth club, fifty-fifty white and black. Lots of youngsters came and eventually we had to transfer it to the parish hall - the "Allardyce" - which was not centrally located.

Fine an idea as a mixed race youth club was, we found by stages that the human choices went another way. After very few months, the Friday night club at the Allardyce was all black and we had to start a Wednesday night alternative for our white youngsters. The two racial groups didn't hate each other; it was simply the case that the music and the style were different. A little while afterwards the YCW set up a disco on Friday nights in the crypt of the large central Anglican church. It did not compete with the Friday Allardyce club; its clientele was completely white. All this was an early lesson in racial dynamics.

Both Friday and Wednesday night clubs flourished, the Friday one especially so. Twenty-five years later, its early members were still holding reunions with each other and their original mentors. Most of the lads - there were many more boys than girls - were pupils at Tulse Hill Boys School. At this time the School accommodated two thousand boys in a single giant "slab block" and was known as "the boy factory". It was a tough institution but nevertheless those who survived the turmoil of the lower years did come under the influence of some very good teachers. The veterans of Friday nights at the Allardyce regard the Club and Tulse Hill School as the twin formative influences in their lives. Together, they helped raise black consciousness, lifted horizons and gave the lads belief in themselves. The leadership of the Club was shared between a remarkable girl of Anglo-Irish parentage who later

11

- having retrained from a laboratory technician to a teacher - became a deputy head of Tulse Hill School. She worked in partnership with my fellow curate, an Irishman, who also did a little teaching at Tulse Hill.

In addition to the music, the Club developed football and cricket teams and there were two epic summer holiday trips by mini-bus to Spain and Morocco. One memorable Easter Monday evening after some of us had been on a country ramble, we all repaired to the Allardyce for "Music City", a disco night. Some three hundred or more young black boys and girls packed into the hall that night and the whole place shook to reggae music. The event was managed by a team of six people, including us two priests and a black lady we had drafted in to help at the door. The evening was roaring away, successfully enough, when a group of strange boys "jumped" the girl who was doing solo service in the refreshment room. These lads grabbed the takings and made for the door. They crashed through the exit doors with one of the priests hanging onto the coat tails of the last of them. The other priest (me) joined in the fray and between us we managed to apprehend our man and get him back into the hall protesting his innocence. The police were slow in coming and before they arrived the others missed their pal and came back to look for him. We lost our prisoner in the ensuing mêlée.

On another of these Bank Holiday excursions, a mixed crowd of us - young and older, boys and girls, black and white - finished up in a pub in Dorking. We were in the process of ordering our drinks from the barman when the manager stepped into the bar and said, "don't serve them!". This infuriated some of the lads, especially the black ones, and we all made our protestations. The manager was adamant so we began to flounce out. As we did so, one of the black lads smashed a panel of glass in the door. Two of us who were responsible for the group emptied our loose change onto the bar towards the cost of the glass. We then joined the rest of the group outside, all seething with anger. They had no doubt that it was racist rejection on the part of the manager.

The next day, I wrote to the manager asking him if he had turned us down because some of our party were under age or because some of them were black. When I received no answer, I referred the matter to the Commission for Racial Equality, the watchdog body that had been set up under our first law against racial discrimination. A young black adjudicator came to see me and agreed to take up the case. I had a copy of the letter I had written to the manager but he denied ever having received it. The brewers who owned the pub acted with alacrity disclaiming all anti-black dispositions and apologising for the embarrassment caused. We were content to leave it at that, satisfied that we had exercised the law in favour of our lad. But we did not congratulate him on breaking the glass.

As already noted the Allardyce lads were still holding reunions twenty-five years later. The most recent one was held in a wine bar in Brixton owned by one of them which has a gallery of African and Caribbean art in an upstairs room. Another member used to have an exotic hat shop in the same road. The convener of the reunion was a management consultant having previously been a youth leader. A further one of their number had been a teacher at Tulse Hill but sadly he had died while still in his thirties.

Race relations in Lambeth

These years also saw the formation of the Lambeth Council for Community Relations, the CCR. There had been some early official attempts at multi-racial encounter promoted by the Council. These were generally dances at the Town Hall with ethnic food available and they were likely to be graced by West Indian representatives from the newly created High Commissions in London. The launching of the CCR, however, was a more determined effort to promote racial harmony and it was to become a permanent feature of Lambeth life until it ran into financial trouble in the late eighties and the shell of its organisation returned to Lambeth Council. In the late sixties, the Lambeth CCR, one of the first in the field, mobilised a great deal of good will and honest effort. The various Christian churches were well to the fore and the first elected chairman was an Anglican vicar. The public reputation of the churches was high in those days and on the whole has remained so. Borough councillors were also prominent, the trade unions too including the National Union of Teachers whose representative was a ferocious communist. There were not very many black organisations then but a considerable number of black people attended the meetings.

Shortly after its inception, a full-time Community Relations Officer was appointed. This was George Greaves, a Guyanese, who had served in the RAF during the Second World War. He did a very notable job in Lambeth for the next twenty years through many strains and disasters. At first he was a council appointee but he gradually detached himself and his organisation from council control. In the best years, George Greaves was at the centre of a network of projects and activities, some more successful than others, but all signifying a determined attempt to advance the welfare and development of ethnic communities. Community centres were

14

set up, also various kinds of youth provision including hostels for the young homeless and a "help on arrest" scheme by which selected adults could be summoned to stand in loco parentis for youngsters who would otherwise be bereft of help. There was also a much needed advice service and support for individuals in pursuit of justice. Antagonism between the police and the black community was already an incipient problem. The CCR made early attempts to sweeten the relationship.

At this time, race relations in Brixton were reasonably harmonious. All sorts of constructive dialogues were going on - in schools, in the social services, in church circles, with employers and with the police. Notting Hill was much more of a racial trouble spot. There had been an ugly disturbance when the police had tried to make arrests for illegal drinking at a café frequented by black men. There were also worrying reports that Notting Hill harboured "Black Power" activity imported from America. This phenomenon, which we scarcely understood, suddenly appeared in Brixton and on our parish patch. An officer from the special branch of the police came to the parish house one morning. The parish priest was ill in hospital at the time and it fell to me to cope with the situation which ensued. The officer had a leaflet with him advertising a Black Power meeting in the Allardyce Hall - did we know about it? A rapid enquiry with the parishioner who handled the hall bookings yielded the information that an unknown person had booked the hall for a "black cultural evening". Further consultations with the police, the Diocese and our solicitor determined that we both could and should cancel the booking. Notices to this effect were posted at the hall and a cancellation letter was delivered to the address of the person who had actually made the booking. This brought the actual managers of the event - some heavy black Americans - to the presbytery and I and my fellow curate had a very sticky session of recriminations.

At the time, we were content that we had managed to keep Black Power at bay in Lambeth. Subsequently we agreed that we had probably been over-anxious and over-persuaded by the police. Political agitation on behalf of black people was bound to come to Britain and it was probably wiser to give it an open forum. Certainly in later years race relations in Brixton did become heavily politicised though not quite in the mode of such people as Malcolm X and Angela Davies in America. Our little ban at the Allardyce Hall was not much more than temporary deflection of the trend of events.

But if political agitation and civil disturbance were still to come, a whole range of social conditioning factors were already well in evidence. The housing situation in Lambeth was desperate. People were constantly moving into an already over-crowded borough. The chief housing officer (a very good man who moved from Lambeth to tackle the housing problems of Belfast) declared that a determined and well resourced attack on the housing problems of the borough could only hope to make the situation in twenty years time no worse than it was at the time he spoke. A large part of the housing stock was still in its pre-1939 condition and a large part of it was in multi-occupation. Most black people inhabited the private sector and were struggling to pay either rent or mortgage payments. A lot of white people were moving away from the area and it was the newcomers who took over their houses. Certain estate agents perceived the new market and made a lot of money out of the people's necessity. Looking back, quite a number of black house owners congratulated themselves on buying comparatively cheaply in the sixties. Perhaps they had forgotten what the price felt like at the time and what a strain it was to keep up the payments. Not very many black families were housed in the public sector at this time. With long waiting lists going back a number of years, black families only gradually became eligible for Council accommodation. This picture has changed radically since.

From the parish perspective, one became aware of some excruciating housing need nearly every week. In an effort to make a dent in the problem, a group of us - Corpus Christi parishioners and some members of the large central Anglican church, St Matthew's, got together to form the Tate Housing Association. Voluntary housing schemes were getting a good deal of government encouragement at the time. We chose "Tate" for our title because the central Brixton library bore the name - that of a 19th century benefactor in the borough - and we thought he would give us excellent local credentials too. The Lambeth housing department was marvellously co-operative - amazingly so seeing that we had nothing to offer except good will and a readiness to work at it. A friend of mine gave us £1,000 for our initial expenses; thereafter the Council advanced us considerable sums to buy and convert the two houses that became our stock.

Our model for the task was the recently formed Catholic Housing Aid Society (CHAS) which had been started by a Catholic priest who later became a bishop in Ireland. His field of operations was North London and he was unwilling to expand into South London. His advice was to plunge into the task - we could learn in the doing of it. We made a ludicrous start by getting mixed up with a group of sharks whose know-how we fondly coveted and who deftly manipulated us for their own ends. But when we managed to detach ourselves from them, we began to make progress. We had regular meetings in the home of one of our number. These meetings were sometimes hilarious and sometimes very fraught.

I was the one who looked for the houses and who negotiated with the housing department. The two houses we managed to acquire and convert yielded seven "units" of housing ranging from a three-bedroomed flat to a commodious bed-sitter. Once the places were occupied, members of the committee set to as rent collectors, maintenance hands and welfare officers. We had all the problems endemic in the housing business. We had bad payers, tenants who couldn't get on with each other, blocked drains, loose tiles and, with grotesque ill fortune, water from a burst main some way up the street from one of our houses by-passed several of our neighbours in order to inundate our basement flat.

But we made a contribution. Roughly two years after we began, I was posted to another parish. In the parochial ministry it is no good pleading that the work you are doing is too important to leave. I tried to keep up my role in the housing association from my new station but it was a forlorn hope. I was no longer in a position to comb the streets for houses to buy and so we were unlikely to grow. The others contemplated lifetimes of rent collecting, tenant soothing and crisis managing, so we decided to bequeath our assets and responsibilities to one of the larger housing associations that were now working south of the river. We managed to complete our affairs tidily and with a reasonable cash balance. So we went out of business. All of us concerned have tender memories of it but I hold the only material relic. This is an estate agent's-type board emblazoned with the name of the Tate which was carefully painted for us by the daughter of one of our committee members.

Mention has already been made of the early signs of a homelessness problem among young black lads. The Brixton Hostel Project was an attempt at a response. This time the zealots were an ecumenical group of clergy and some lay people, including the senior careers officer for Brixton. While I was having driving lessons with a school on Brixton Hill, the head of the firm, my instructor, told me that a young black lad they employed had taken to sleeping in the cars at night. It transpired that the boy did not get on with his step-father and had taken off from home. Comparing notes with other local clergy, it became apparent that there was a growing problem of homelessness among the young. The staff at Tulse Hill School confirmed it. Further evidence came to light when I found a black lad hiding in the Church when I went to lock it one night.

The Hostel Project was meant to address simply the problem of homelessness. We never meant to take on disturbed lads or those in trouble with the law. We aspired to provide a temporary home for youngsters who had nowhere safe to live and whose lives were otherwise viable. Again a long negotiation with Lambeth Council ensued, this time with the social services and architects departments, and again councillors and officers were very co-operative. We found a large house at Tulse Hill suitable for the purpose which could accommodate a dozen or fifteen boys. We had to go through all the planning hoops - the statutory amount of bed-space for each resident, fire precautions, the right sort of staff accommodation and much else. The Council duly advanced us the money to buy and convert the house. Some of us on the committee spent a lot of time trying to involve Dr Barnados in the Project. We really needed such a partner. Finding, maintaining and relieving staff in residential homes requires a great deal of expertise and resources. Dr Barnados were interested and willing to come in with us but we came to grief on the condition that they then required that the warden should be an evangelical Christian. Most of our committee were unwilling to accept this and we decided to go ahead alone.

We were most unwise. We appointed as warden a young black man who looked promising but the choice was really an error in "positive discrimination". We compounded our mistake by taking on a lot of boys on remand from the courts, contrary to our original intention. These lads had maintenance grants behind them and their money helped to pay our considerable running costs. Such lads were not easy to handle and soon proved to be beyond the scope of our young warden and his volunteer assistants. Within a year, the hostel had become unmanageable. The Council repossessed the premises with the intention of reopening them after a while for the same purpose. The rump of the committee who were also trustees had a humiliating interview with our bank manager who eventually agreed in a lordly fashion to ask his head office to write-off our debts of several thousand pounds.

Though our Project failed, there was no doubt about the need for such hostels. We were an early attempt to meet it. In the years that followed, a great deal of public money was poured into hostel schemes and some of them collapsed even more resoundingly than ours did.

Ministrations in Brixton Prison

For the first two years of my time at Corpus Christi, the parish was still responsible for pastoral care in the Prison. After this time a full-time Catholic priest was appointed to parallel the Anglican chaplain who also had an assistant. I used to spend most of Wednesdays circulating among the prisoners and staff and would put in other appearances too, as would my fellow curate. At this time, there was a shifting population of inmates of about a thousand of which a quarter would be Catholics. In doing occasional parish appeals for the Catholic Prisoners Social Service (now The Bourne Trust), I used to say that most of the hard men in Brixton were English and protestant and the minor and amiable offenders were Irish and Catholic. (These were pre-Provisional IRA days). It was an unserious remark, there being far too many exceptions, but it was true that for many inmates prison was entirely inappropriate treatment. There were lots of psychiatric cases which called for treatment more than punishment, and lots of trivial offenders for whom fines would have been adequate correction. A stateless individual was there for no other reason that having fallen ill while serving on a ship in the port of London, when the time came for him to be released from hospital, his ship having left, he had to be prevented from melting into the populace as an illegal immigrant. Mercifully, his shipping company supplied him with all the comforts that the prison authorities would allow in and eventually the Brazilian government gave him citizenship.

There were very few black prisoners at this time. By the nineties, a very large proportion of the total prison population was black. But probably in the sixties, the black component in institutions for young people was already increasing. It is well known that Britain incarcerates more people than any other European country. Have we succeeded in criminalising a lot of black people who would have been law abiding citizens in their countries of origin? By far the biggest number of black offenders are among those who were born or who had their early upbringing here and there can scarcely be a doubt that black crime is a facet of poor race relations. As a nation we have done far too little to give young blacks a proper stake in society. The anger that erupted in the Brixton disturbances of 1981 and 1985 was the cry of those who felt ill-regarded and oppressed. We have to discuss those dismaying events and their implications later. For the moment it is worth our while to note that black crime and especially street crime has been described usefully as a slow form of riot. This is not the whole truth and it is probably becoming less of a truth. But it can help to point us in the direction of a remedy. As a society we have to learn to value our young people and especially our black young people far more and bend great efforts to see that the education system works for them and that they find training and opportunity when they leave school.

The Railton Road area was already taking on the ambience of Kingston, Jamaica, transposed into the grey streets of London. Railton Road was the spine of black settlement in Brixton. The streets around had plenty of working class families of many races who were struggling to keep their heads above water and to bring up their children decently. But there were a number of drinking dives, a good deal of trafficking in "ganja" (cannabis) and a certain amount of prostitution. These features became greatly aggravated in later years when the whole area became known as the "Front

Line". It was the area in which the disturbances of 1981 and 1985 gestated.

Decay and overcrowding were the manifest evils of the sixties and there were very many hidden distresses. There were African students labouring to qualify, single mothers with young children surviving somehow, elderly white people engulfed by the newcomers around them, young adults of various colours holed up in squalid drug pads. In the summer, there was the parade of life in the streets. The pubs spilled out their customers onto the streets, sugar cane was on sale in Railton Road so was carrot juice. Music shops blasted out soul, reggae and calypso as if everyone around was stone deaf. On the corners groups of men would be "liming" (a Trinidad expression for hanging around and chatting) and some of them would be ready to accommodate a customer in the ganja market.

Brixton overall had a tremendous personality. Even in its worst days the "Front Line" area was ambiguous. On the one hand it seethed with crime and on the other it was the community belonging for a lot of men who would otherwise have been ducks without water. A lot of black men "smoked" - that is they smoked ganja. Hard drugs began to be traded in but most of the customers to begin with were incoming white youngsters. In the eighties, some black men and women acquired a cocaine habit. Violence often threatened but it had not yet got out of hand. The practice of carrying knives had already begun, especially on the part of young black men. Most of the casualties of knife attacks were other black youngsters. Later on, I was to conduct the funerals of a number of victims of knife attacks and I took to giving out solemn warnings on the evil of carrying knives. I happened to be in a street near Railton Road one afternoon when two young fellows clashed in the middle of the road. They broke off and grabbed a dustbin lid each and then one saw that each had a knife in the other hand. They clashed again and one boy was cut across the back of his hand and the other received a wound in his stomach. One of them took refuge in a house. The other would certainly have killed him if he could have got at him. Some months after, I met the boy with the stomach wound in the street and felt sufficiently concerned to warn him that he could have killed his opponent that afternoon. He shrugged his shoulders and said, "we're friends again now".

Remarkably, race relations between ethnic communities in central Brixton have always been reasonably harmonious, in contrast to the relationship between young blacks and the police. Brixton never became a black ghetto like certain districts of many American cities. Even at the time of the nineteen-eighties riots, white people were in a small majority in central Brixton. A lot of the white people were elderly, however, and most of their black neighbours were young and vigorous. White and black people shared the same deprivations but at the same time there were a lot of solid working-class families of all races who were buying their houses and sprucing them up. These made up the core of the population and they had no interest in lawlessness and riot. Later when the Victoria Line of the Underground was extended to Brixton, central Brixton became a desirable area for "yuppies". Another inducement for the upwardly mobile was that the houses were cheap. Towards the Herne Hill end of Railton Road, the streets of "poets' corner" branch off. These are Chaucer, Spenser, Shakespeare and Milton Roads and they contain some interesting old houses, in price well below the Hampstead and Dulwich levels. By the eighties these had attracted quite a few media and literary people in spite of the fact that the Front Line was only a short step away.

In the late sixties, some black families had already prospered enough to move away from Brixton. West Norwood and Thornton Heath were the desirable districts. This exodus gathered momentum with the years. Brixton became synonymous with trouble and deprivation and many people wanted to leave that behind.

Towards what proved to be the end of my time in Corpus Christi, I, with others, began to petition our Archbishop about the pastoral needs of our black community. It was clear enough at that time that our parishes were not catering adequately for black Catholics. We were not attracting them to Church and we scarcely understood their struggles. Already black Pentecostal congregations were springing up and we did not even realise that we were losing a lot of our people to them. In my view, the black community represented a particular pastoral need which was also a great pastoral opportunity. I had never met a black person who did not believe in God or reverence the name of Christ. They needed a priest of their own - ideally, perhaps, a West Indian one who also understood the London scene. But failing that, a white one would have to learn enough about the people to care for them effectively. By implication, I was volunteering for the job.

There was already a white priest working among the black community in Westminster Diocese across the river. He had previously been a missionary in South America. There was also a small network of priests who had different kinds of involvements with black people in various parts of the country. Several were parish clergy, one was a field worker with the nascent Catholic Commission for Racial Justice, another was a religious order priest who had a distinguished career as a chaplain to an African university. We used to meet a couple of times a year in Coventry under the chairmanship of Bishop Joseph Cleary, one of the auxiliary bishops of Birmingham Diocese, who was the first at the episcopal level to show concern for ethnic issues.

However, it took our Diocese several years to come round to the idea. In the meantime, I was posted to another parish on the margins of Kent where I stayed for the next three years - from the summer of 1970 until the summer of 1973. These proved to be very good years too in a very different

24

way. Nevertheless, I stayed with the idea of a specialised ministry to our black community and when I was elected to the Diocesan Council of Priests, one of the new consultative bodies that was taking shape in the Catholic Church, I ran the cause among a very varied assembly of my fellow clergy and in the presence of the Archbishop. The upshot was that in the summer of 1973 I was appointed "chaplain to the immigrants" throughout the Diocese. My first task was to write my own job description.

A Caribbean representative brings up the gifts at an annual multi-cultural Mass at St George's Cathedral, Southwark.

Specialised ministry - the beginnings

Before I was expressly told that I was to be "chaplain to immigrants" in the Diocese - there was just a murmur to this effect going around - I received an approach from the national headquarters of the Young Christian Workers in Kennington, South London. The Movement was looking for a new national chaplain - would I let my name go forward to the Archbishop and, if he was agreeable, to the Bishops Conference who would make the actual appointment? My Brixton experience had made me a great enthusiast for the YCW. Although my section there had not taken part significantly in my contacts with black people, I now knew enough about YCW method to understand how effective it could be as "lay apostle" training for ordinary boys and girls on the margins of the Church community.

I have already described how the Brixton YCW's public meeting on the recreational needs of young people was a key factor in the launch of the Allardyce youth clubs. Another of its achievements was a project to finance a fresh water supply for a village in India. We had been advised by the Catholic Fund for Overseas Development (CAFOD) that drilling for water and the provision of a communal pump was a prime need for countless villages in India. This, our YCW boys and girls thought, was a very specific and manageable project - it would cost about £500 - and, apart from the money raising, it would help to increase awareness about the needs of the Third World. We set up an exhibition showing what a transformation a good water supply could make in an Indian village and CAFOD even gave us the name of the village we would help and its location on the map. The parish had the benefit of the exhibition to begin with and then (with permission) we transferred it to the Lambeth Central Library. The money came in easily and the boys and girls were thrilled

The money came in easily and the boys and girls were thrilled with their success.

Good an undertaking as this was and valuable too as a confidence booster for our youngsters, it was still something less than fundamental YCW work. We really needed to probe more deeply into the life situation of our own young people, white and black. As we have seen, this process began to happen with the black lads of the Friday night youth club and of Tulse Hill School. Later on, we did manage to get an effective black YCW network going with notable results. Curiously, though the Brixton YCW did not have black participation, it did attract a considerable fringe of Greek lads. Some of these came more for the girls than anything else but they were a means by which we developed links with the Greek Orthodox community which had a church not too far away at Camberwell Green.

The Brixton YCW did produce some excellent young apostles. One of our early leaders became a missionary priest in South America. Several became teachers and one an active trade unionist.

Dual ministry

Though I still had a great deal to learn, the prospect of working with the YCW at the national level was very attractive to me. When asked by YCW headquarters if I could be available, the Archbishop of Southwark duly said that I was already earmarked for work with the "immigrants". I asked if I could be allowed to do both. The Archbishop agreed reluctantly and in October, 1973, I acquired two new jobs - national chaplain to the YCW and "chaplain to the immigrants" of Southwark Diocese.

To begin with, I spent most of my time with the YCW. There was a role to take up in the national team of eight highly energetic and strong-minded full-time "organisers". These were young men and women who had proved

28

themselves through local sections and regional teams and were now working for the Movement full-time at the national level. As national chaplain, I had administrative and writing responsibilities at the headquarters and there was a whole pattern of events to take part in and visits to be made throughout the country. I used to spend a great deal of time on the road, always accompanied by at least one of my comrades in the national team. At the peak, I was driving at least 20,000 miles a year.

I felt at the time that I had energy enough for the two jobs. It is a question, though, if I was wise to try and run the two together. Some of my black friends reproached me for the amount of time I gave to the YCW and sometimes my YCW comrades would refer to me as their "part-time" chaplain. The balance tilted as time went on. At the end of my five years with the YCW, I concentrated on a few specific duties and scarcely left London. Fortunately there was a second priest in the team by then who took on more and more of the strain and eventually he succeeded me. But my experience of the YCW was to prove a key part of my education for my work with the black community. It committed me thoroughly to the Lay Apostolate. I learned the principle of "like to like": that just as young workers were the first and best apostles of other young workers, so black people were the best apostles of other black people. In all the subsequent work I did in the black community I depended almost completely on lay collaborators.

I went to live in the parish of West Wandsworth where one of my predecessors in the YCW was parish priest. He became a very good friend despite the fact that my peculiar comings and goings and my occupation of the telephone were a great trial to him.

I began my work with the black community at weekends - at least the weekends when I was not elsewhere on YCW business. But first, I had to consider what should be my scope. I rapidly came to the conclusion that I would have to devote myself to the Caribbean community. I had had some experience of West Indian people in Brixton and they were the biggest single ethnic group in South London and in the country at large. However, from the beginning I made friends with Africans and Asians and these grew in numbers with the passing of the years.

Opening moves in the South East

My earliest operations had a South-East and a South-West reference. In the South-East - the Peckham and East Dulwich area - I met two very active St Lucian laymen through the priest who was already functioning with the West Indian community in Westminster Diocese. They were helping him with the links that he had in South London. John Bonaparte and Charles Gaillard immediately welcomed me and became my close collaborators. John was in his early thirties and Charles a little older. Neither of them was married at that time. Both had aspired to the priesthood while still young men in St Lucia and both had begun training. John had joined the "Fils de Marie Immaculée", the "FMIs", the French missionary order which had looked after St Lucia and also Dominica for over one hundred years.

However, John was not happy in the novitiate in France and he came to London where he took a job with the Post Office. Charles also worked for the Post Office in London. He had wanted to be a Benedictine but that too had not been a happy experience. He had not felt fully accepted at the mother house in France where he was sent for training. In spite of these disappointments, both John and Charles remained ardent Catholics. Subsequently, both were ordained permanent deacons in Southwark Diocese, Charles in 1986 and John in 1991, and at the time of writing, Charles is doing further studies with a view to being ordained a priest for service back home in St Lucia. John married in 1982 and has a young son who was one of the servers at his father's ordination.

At the time I first got to know them, John and Charles were both active laymen and catechists in the parish of St James, Peckham. When I came on to the scene, they both took me round to meet black Catholic families in the area, most of them St Lucians. I discovered how powerful were kinship and community ties from home. Family events would bring together people from anywhere in London and indeed from Luton and even Birmingham. I was gradually moving into the milieu of the black community and the pastoral maps were vastly different from those of the parochial clergy. Though I tried to resist the calls, I found that I could not avoid visiting, saying house masses, conducting weddings and taking part in funerals all over London. Happily, I never received any rebuffs from the local clergy when I operated outside my own territory.

Introductions with John and Charles were my entrée into the St Lucian community. The Saturday afternoon visits went on steadily and then I remembered the value of the house masses we had in Brixton. So together we initiated another series of house masses, nearly always on Saturday nights. These became more and more West Indian in flavour. We always sang, we had spontaneous prayers but with the informality there was always solemnity and deep devotion. It was remarkable really how this was achieved. The living rooms were invariably packed with people overflowing into the passage ways, the floor would be covered with children and distributing Holy Communion was sometimes a slightly precarious business. Sometimes, we would precede the mass with confessions in a back room or an upstairs bedroom. After the mass there would be drinks and a lot to eat. Before long I was well inducted into the cuisine of the West Indies. However, there were two items that I never learned to like. One was black pudding straight out of the pot and the other was a great West Indian delicacy, "souse", boiled pigs trotter. My friends used to laugh with pity at my inability to appreciate some of their most succulent dishes.

By stages we began to build up a sense of Catholic community. The next move was to start an organisation. The South-East London West Indian Catholic Organisation (SELWICO) took shape in the home of Mr and Mrs Felton Joseph in Crystal Palace Road, East Dulwich. The actual launch took place in February, 1975, with Father Paul Gouraud, an FMI father, in attendance. Father Paul was visiting St Lucian families in London during his European leave from the West Indies. SELWICO was about to be born when it became possible for me to pay my first visit to the Caribbean from January to March in 1975. By the time I returned, the organisation was fledged.

SELWICO people were all in work at this time, mostly factory work or construction for the men. Nearly all the womenfolk had jobs too - hospital or canteen work, assistants in old peoples homes and a few did child-minding. Child care for women at work tended to be a constant problem. There were never enough places in the Council nurseries and payments for child minders made a big hole in women's earnings. In the West Indies, there was nearly always a grandmother to look after the children of working mothers. The lack of extended family was one of the features of life back home that our people in London missed most.

The first task of SELWICO was to draw up a statement of its purpose. We decided that we were in business to encourage the practice of the Faith among West Indian (not only St Lucian) Catholics. We were to organise social events to gather our people together. We wanted to relieve distresses in our community and to raise money to help the people back home, especially for education. Committee meetings took place monthly at the Josephs. Mrs Joseph had a grand-daughter, Sasha, born about this time. I always thought of Sasha as SELWICO's mascot. She was always on somebody's lap at committee meetings, and a picture of her on my lap appeared with the first article about us in a Catholic publication.

We began to organise dances and sea-side outings. Taking a deep breath, we booked the North Peckham Civic Centre for our first big dance. The centre was quite expensive and we had to have a band that wasn't cheap but we need not have worried. This first dance and the subsequent ones drew in hundreds of people. We watched the bar, run by a local licensee in arrangement with Southwark Council, do good business and resented the fact that this money wasn't coming our way. Another of our griefs was the early closure time determined by the Council. This was 11.30pm. For West Indian people this would have been more like a starting time. Our dances used to fill up after 10pm and at 11pm they would be going full blast. Later on, we tried a few dances at a rather shabby church hall that had a 2am closure time. This was better for time and we did run the bar ourselves and collect the profits. But we missed the Civic Centre which was much smarter. SELWICO never did succeed in having it both ways.

Our sea-side outings were a great success. We never had any trouble in filling a coach and sometimes we would need two. The formula was an early start from the Peckham Bus Garage and then the open road for somewhere on the coast. We patronised all the main South Coast resorts over the years and we got especially attached to Clacton on the East Coast where we went three times. I took to arranging with the Catholic parish for a mass around midday and if possible the use of the hall afterwards. This nearly always worked and we had some very friendly welcomes, especially at Clacton. This made up for the weather there which was nearly always brisk and chilly. We would generally do a fair amount of drinking during the day though I don't ever remember anyone the worse for wear. The youngsters would look for the fun fair; scarcely ever would anyone go for a bathe in the sea. All our people, including the youngsters born in Britain, had strictly Caribbean standards for what constitutes good beaches and good bathing. A central feature of any outing would be a succulent picnic with chicken, savoury meat dishes, rice and mixed vegetables and many other accompaniments. Coming home was always splendidly cheerful. There would be singing, music and often dancing in the aisle of the coach.

We also began to celebrate St Lucy's Day each December on the Saturday evening nearest the actual date, December 13th. We had mass generally at St James', Peckham, followed by a family social in the hall. It was always one of my jobs to negotiate an occasional licence for the bar. In December, 1977, we spread our wings and held our St Lucy's Day mass at St George's cathedral with our new Archbishop, Monsignor Michael Bowen, as Chief Concelebrant, and Mr David Lane, head of the Commission for Racial Equality, as guest of honour. I was very on edge wondering whether our people would find their way to the cathedral which was unfamiliar to nearly all of them and sure enough the congregation was very sparse when we began. But people kept on arriving all during the mass and when we had finished the Archbishop murmured encouragingly, "there were a lot of people at the end".

South West developments

First in time was my encounter with a group of families mainly from Dominica - in the Wandsworth/Wimbledon area of South West London. I met them through a relative of one of them who was present at a mass I celebrated at the Fraternity of the Little Sisters of Jesus at Fulham. We took to each other at once and became great friends. This is sad to relate because later we fell out and our activities gradually came to an end. But this unhappy conclusion does not quench the pleasure and value of much that we did together.

As in the South East, we began with a series of house masses on Saturday evenings, going round to each family in turn. I met a lot of new people this way, quite a few of them from North London. The Dominican linkages were even more London-wide than the St Lucian. Gradually other West Indian homelands came into the picture. Two families from Guyana

- related to each other - became closely involved and we gathered in some South West St Lucians.

Most of the group - not all - were in good jobs. They all had lovely children, some in the late teens, and these were very much part of our proceedings. We had scarcely completed a round of house masses when they all wanted to form an organisation and develop a mission. We chose the title "South West London Catholic Caribbean Council" (SWLCCC). Our purpose was strongly Christian. As with SELWICO (though the SWLCCC was first in the field) we wanted to create a vibrant sense of Christian community. Social activities were going to be important - again we needed to bring our people together - and SWLCCC also aspired to be a voice for the Caribbean community in matters of justice. We designed a badge and a logo for our notepaper, as did SELWICO a little later. So in both organisations we had purpose and enthusiasm.

Dances in the South West began to be organised a little earlier than in the South East and they gradually became more ambitious. We began in Fulham Town Hall with the same time limitation that SELWICO chafed at in the North Peckham Civic Centre. The first one threatened to end in a big row when one of the Council officials had the stupidity and the effrontery to pull the plug out on the sound system on the dot of closing time. Our band was "The Blue Wonders" who often played for us in the years that followed in both the South East and the South West. The great "everybody-on-the-floor" number at this time was "Grenada, may God bless you". Later it was "Hot, hot, hot". I became thoroughly addicted to West Indian music - calypso, soca, reggae, soul and all the enormously inventive variations. A difference gradually opened up between what pleased the youngsters and what suited the oldsters. But at this early stage all the music seemed exciting, compelling movement. For a white person, I could move reasonably well but I often found myself watching our people's natural sense of rhythm with delight and sometimes - when real virtuosos were performing - with exhilaration. The SWLCCC moved it's dances to West End hotels eventually. The expenses went up drastically and there was at least one occasion when we looked financial ruin in the face. But we did attract big crowds and the catering was of a very high standard. No one could doubt that our dances were excellent value for money even when the tickets went up to over ten pounds. We probably did get over-ambitious and allowed ourselves to get preoccupied with bigger and better social events to the detriment of our other purposes.

During the time I was in the Abbey Wood parish (after leaving Brixton) we had organised a number of very successful family weekends shared by parents, teenagers and children. We had separate discussion sessions for the adults and appropriate activities for the teenagers and children with a team of young adults looking after them. We all came together for meals, the liturgy and a social evening on the Saturday. Presented with the idea, the South West families were very enthusiastic. Our first event was a weekend at Hengrave Hall, a retreat/conference centre in Suffolk. It was a huge success. We had no difficulty in recruiting the participants; we had a similar programme catering for the different age groups; and all our people were delighted by the welcome we received from the sisters who ran the place. It was a beautiful house with extensive grounds and a farm. The youngsters found plenty to do with their free time and the adults enjoyed the programme we had planned and felt relaxed and wanted.

The next time, we had a five-day summer holiday again at Hengrave Hall. It was another excellent event - on this occasion we played lots of cricket, including "a match" with some YCW boys we happened to coincide with. Our players were a faithful reflection of the supremacy of the West Indies test team, especially some of our young mums who were very stylish at the crease. One, indeed, had played in the Guyana women's team. We again had some serious Christian discussions. I remember one particularly good session on family limitation, contraception and related matters.

Our third visit to Hengrave was not so good. The weather was dreadful and we had great difficulty in keeping our youngsters occupied and out of trouble. Our programme was much too sketchy and we felt less approved of by the Hengrave community. It was a shame that it was a disappointment because several South East families came to this one - it was our first joint venture. And if it had been as good as our previous visits, we would probably have embarked on some more ambitious projects.

All the time I was wanting to get YCW going with our over sixteens. We had four such lads among the South West families, all relatives or close friends with each other. Very early on, I managed to persuade them to come to a London YCW weekend at Haywards Heath. All the rest of the forty or so participants were white boys and girls. They gave my four a very warm welcome but to begin with it was clear that we had a chalk and cheese situation on our hands. My lads, of course, had mixed with white youngsters at school but there was no mistaking the fact that when they had the choice they would always choose other black company. This kind of voluntary separation was very much the rule in the sixties and seventies and, as we saw in connection with the youth clubs in Brixton, it did not necessarily imply hostility towards white or any other species of young people. Nevertheless in differentiating itself, any such group is bound to measure itself against others and develop a language and attitudes about them. By the end of this particular YCW weekend, however, my four lads were really mixing in with everyone else and showing evident signs of enjoying themselves.

The Haywards Heath weekend intrigued the lads sufficiently to make them ready to meet regularly and to try and get some of their black friends involved. We did a number of good enquiries into the situation of black youth in

Britain. There was no doubt that they felt very much on the outside looking in and these were boys who were getting reasonably well-educated and had plenty of parental encouragement. They were all quite sure that they had to be twice as good as their white counterparts to get an equivalent job. The prospects for a promising YCW group looked good but we were beaten by the irregularity of my participation due to my absences on national YCW business. I tried to get another priest to be their chaplain in my stead but alas he did not come through. At this stage of development they needed a lot of encouragement.

The story of our whole South West operation was one of great promise and great disappointment. And I think too, failure on my part. We fell out eventually over the control of the house the Diocese acquired for us in 1977. We had wanted a centre for some time - it was the logical next step to the organisations that we had formed. Earlier we had looked at places in South East London but at that time the Diocese was not ready to jump. We were not sure to begin with about what sort of premises we were looking for. Did we want a club sort of set-up where we could have our social events? How about acquiring a redundant church with house and hall attached? Would a large house be sufficient where I would live and maybe provide a home for others and where we would have some rooms large enough for meetings. Whatever we chose, what would be the best location? The Clapham Common area suggested itself. It was roughly in the centre of South London with good communications. And it was on the 37 bus route which connected nearly all the places where our people lived.

I am not sure that we got the perfect answer. If we had pursued the church-complex solution, we would have moved on to Sunday worship, drawing black Catholics away from the parishes in which they lived. At this time, as we have seen, the Catholic parishes were not doing very well in attracting their black parishioners. If we had gone down that road, we would probably have attracted a lot of people, as the development of the black Pentecostal congregations would indicate. We would also have been open to the charge, levelled by a number of parish clergy at the time that the chaplaincy was first talked about, that we were intent on setting up a separate black Catholic Church. In the event my key collaborators did not want a separate worshipping centre. They felt that our long term objective was to encourage the participation of black Catholics in their home parishes. The Birmingham chaplaincy chose a different answer. They took over half a redundant school part of which became their Church and the rest their social centre. The priest lived in a house some way away. In the early nineteen-nineties, it is difficult to know where the balance of wisdom lay. Certainly in South London, black participation in parish life had improved very notably. I think our chaplaincy has been a catalyst for this. At the same time, the Birmingham chaplaincy and centre has established a very vibrant black Catholic community but maybe it has been less of an influence on the Diocesan community as a whole.

A six-bedroomed house suddenly became available in Balham. The sisters of the Holy Family of Bordeaux had a small community there but they had decided to shift their work to the new town of Milton Keynes. They were happy that the house should be a centre for the black community and to encourage the idea they were prepared to sell it to the Diocese for a very preferential price and to leave behind a lot of furniture. It was located on the wrong side of Clapham Common and the immediate neighbourhood was slightly up-market. The availability of 135 Nightingale Lane, SW12, settled the issue of what sort of a centre we should choose. The Diocese was prepared to invest in this house; it would be a residence for me and could accommodate several others; it was large enough to have committee and other group meetings there. SELWICO and SWLCCC both agreed that we should take the offer, though the latter was more keen than the former, it being on its territory.

Unhappily, we fell out over the house. I took the view that if it was to be my home I would need to make the decisions about who else should live there and how the house should be organised. My SWLCCC friends felt that it was a centre for the black community and therefore should be managed by a joint committee of SELWICO and SWLCCC members with complete right of access. Looking back, the whole contention may simply have been a misunderstanding and with greater forbearance on my part we could have reached a solution. But at that time, I was unwilling to concede the principle of control and I became estranged from my SWLCCC friends. Some of the families continued to take part in chaplaincy affairs and one of its members became a very close collaborator and in due course a national figure in multi-racial development. But the demise of the SWLCCC was a very sad story and one which I have to regard as one of my failures.

First Caribbean visit

This is a convenient point at which to describe my first visit to the West Indies though it took place in January to March 1975, several years before the events just related. It was obvious that I needed to educate myself for the task of ministering to the Caribbean community and this must mean a trip to the West Indies. The earliest opportunity I had of going was over a year from the time of my appointment. I negotiated a ten week absence from my YCW commitments and decided that I needed most to see Trinidad, St Lucia and Dominica, all in the Eastern Caribbean. I wrote to the bishops of these islands and asked if they could help me. I also had lots of relatives of our people in South London to call on. I travelled with a little portable tape recorder so that I could bring back messages. It would have been good to include Jamaica in this first trip but it is a very long way from the Eastern Caribbean and I had neither the time nor the cash to make it. In my second trip in 1981 I went there first and stayed for three weeks. Jamaica apart, Trinidad, St Lucia and Dominica were the homelands of most of my friends in South London up to that time.

I had never been to the tropics before so the first shock was the heat. To begin with, each day felt like living in an oven. I arrived in Port of Spain, Trinidad, just after dusk and missed the priest whom the Archbishop had asked to meet me. I made my way to Archbishop's House instead and so had an early meeting with Monsignor Anthony Pantin, the Archbishop, who was marvellously welcoming and for whom I developed a very high regard. However, I was meant to be in Arima in the centre-north of the island and the next day I made my way there. My host was Father Hilary Clarke (whom I had missed at the airport), parish priest of Santa Rosa which was the centre for a very large Catholic community. Beside the heat, another thing I had to get used to was a very early start to the day. The first Mass was at 6am. and the parish clergy had office hours up to breakfast at about 7.30am. On Sundays there could be an even earlier first Mass at the parish Church because there were several out-stations to get to. Santa Rosa had several of these, including Comuto Junction where Mass was celebrated under somebody's house in splendid country style with chickens clucking round the makeshift altar and the congregation of all ages gathered round on an amazing variety of perches. During my stay in Trinidad, I was drafted in to look after a parish in the south whose priest was away for the weekend. On the Sunday morning the first Mass was 15 miles away at a satellite village and we began it in the dark. By 9.30am, I had said two more masses at the parish Church, both with large congregations.

It was very clear in Trinidad - and the same was to appear in St Lucia and Dominica - that the people flocked to Church on Sundays. And there was always a lot of people too at the early morning Mass on week days. And the Mass was fully participating, with lots of singing on Sundays and with a great sense of occasion. Lay ministries were very much in evidence. Santa Rosa had a large corps of Special Ministers of Holy Communion some of whom would come forward at the end of each Mass to collect the Blessed Sacrament to take to the sick and housebound, all of whom would receive Holy Communion every Sunday. There were also teams of catechists and lay involvement in marriage preparation and pre-baptismal instruction. There were strict rules for parents before their children could be baptised. I took part in a mandatory pre-baptismal instruction which was attended by at least one hundred parents.

Monsignor Pantin was the first Trinidadian Archbishop of Port of Spain. His predecessor had been a redoubtable Irishman, Monsignor Finbarr Ryan, who had the oversight of nearly all the Eastern Caribbean. The old Archbishop died in

Ireland at the time of my visit having retired from the Caribbean some years before. Archbishop Pantin went to Ireland to lead his Funeral Requiem. There was a great Requiem Mass at the cathedral in Port of Spain which I attended. Anthony Pantin's succession to Finbarr Ryan was a watershed in Caribbean Church history. The old Archbishop had presided over a colonial-type Church regime with a preponderance of European missionary priests and sisters and some teaching brothers, nearly all of them from Ireland. He was an autocratic but devoted shepherd of the flock. He expected to be obeyed within the household of Faith and he was very capable too of standing up to British colonial administrators when the circumstances seemed to require it. But he performed two crucial services to the new indigenous Catholic Church soon to be born. He set up a splendid pattern of Catholic secondary schools throughout Trinidad and he created the seminary for the training of native clergy. There was already a considerable group of Trinidadian priests by the time of his retirement and the proportion of native to missionary clergy has been rising steadily ever since. All but one of the English-speaking islands had native bishops by the time of my 1975 visit and though some islands are making more rapid progress than others, the proportion of native clergy is rising everywhere in the West Indies.

In Trinidad, I discovered the wealth of Caribbean liturgical song that was being created. A record "Sing out my Soul" had just been published, the work of nuns and their secondary school pupils which, in my judgement, was both musically exciting and deeply spiritual. I gradually realised that the hymns and songs on the record were part of a broad movement led by Father Garfield Rochard in Trinidad and Father Richard Ho Lung in Jamaica. Shortly after the time of my first visit, annual liturgical summer schools began to be held in Trinidad and later developed in other islands too. Young people from Britain went to some of these and came back thrilled with their discovery of a genuine Caribbean worshipping idiom. Later a collection of Caribbean song compiled by Garfield Rochard and others was published in Britain as a "Caribbean Hymnal". It came into regular use in South London.

From January onwards in Trinidad, "Carnival" looms larger and larger on the horizon. The artistic preparations would have been going on since the previous summer but following Christmas, the sound of steel band music is everywhere and the new calypsos of the year are being heard constantly on the radio. Carnival Day definitively is Shrove Tuesday, the day before Ash Wednesday and the beginning of Lent. It is a feature of Catholic culture; in Jamaica, Barbados and the other islands where the prevailing culture is protestant, they do not have Carnival though they do import the music.

Travelling around the towns and suburbs of Trinidad during the evenings, there was always "pan" music in one's ear and frequently one came across the sources. These were generally large sheds, brilliantly lit with anything from a dozen to thirty men and girls beating out the music from a variety of vividly painted steel drums or sections thereof. With the pans there would be other instruments - ordinary percussion, maracas, clackers and a brake drum played with a steel rod like a triangle. One evening on my way back to Arima with Father Clarke, we came by one of these roadside sheds with the band in full cry. I date my love affair with the steel band from that evening. We stayed watching and listening for nearly an hour. I resolved there and then that we must have one of these in South London.

I also became a student of calypso. Father Clarke and some of his friends took me to three out of the four major "tents". In the days when steel band and calypso were regarded as low life, this sort of music and song was relegated to rough old locations and shabby make-shift marquees. These were the "tents". With the huge growth in popularity of calypso and the development of both musical skills and power of comment on the part of calypsonians, these "tents" had become

44

companies of singers and musicians bearing the name of one of the leading exponents. All the "tents" had a home base - a hall in the environs of Port of Spain - but in the months before Carnival they would go on tour. The pre-eminent calypsonian, "Mighty Sparrow", had his own place, his "Hideaway". Sparrow's great forte was his wit. Some calypsos were very political, some were little sermonettes, some were very risqué, a few were filthy. Sparrow's were often very suggestive but they were always very funny. And his tunes were terrific and so were the band's rendering of them and the backing behind them. It was never easy for a stranger to catch the lyric; it was essential to do so to appreciate the art form. The words were highly idiomatic and without a text or an explanation a stranger was lost. Father Clarke and his friends were surprised at the interest I showed in the calypsos - they were not used to that from a white person. I got very taken with a 1975 calypso called "Dis Nice Place" by Lord Valentine. The drift of the story was that Trinidadians were in a perpetual party mood while great perils and evils were threatening them from all sides. I was captivated by the tune and gradually mastered the words. Father Clarke thought that it was a "calypso for meditation".

Carnival reaches its crescendo the weekend before Shrove Tuesday. The calypso king and queen titles are awarded (most of the leading calypsonians were men but there were always some remarkable women performers like "Calypso Rose" of "Do Dem Back" fame in 1975); there is the "Panorama" competition for the top steel band; and the contest for Carnival King and Queen - these are the two best centre pieces, male and female, in all the "costume bands". "Costume bands" designated large companies of revellers whose costumes all conformed to an overall theme. So a "Food and Drink" theme would include dancers dressed up as bunches of grapes, wine glasses, waiters and waitresses etc and the two most elaborate costumes would be contenders for Carnival King and Queen. The "Mystical Pheasant" of 1981 (my second Carnival visit) lodges in my memory. It was a gorgeous creation about the size of a minibus with shimmering multi-coloured feathers all arranged on an aluminium frame. Every feather quivered as the dancer inside swayed through the streets to the beat of the music. Trinidad has a number of very well known carnival impresarios. These choose the theme for their costume band and determine its artistic composition. Carnival participants join a band and pay for the materials of their costume. Most often the impresario himself and the lady of his choice would dance in the king and queen centre pieces.

Carnival in Trinidad has traditionally been frowned upon by the Church. A spirit of gay abandon is essential to it and this is not always conducive to good morals. But it is now generally recognised as a cultural creation special to the island (only the carnival of Rio de Janeiro in South America challenges it) and it is a huge tourist attraction, now drawing in people from North America and Europe besides the Caribbean and the nearby South American mainland. Later on, the Notting Hill carnival in London comes into our story - its debt to carnival in Trinidad and the attempts made by the Churches to sacralise it.

After the carnival of 1975, I moved on to St Lucia and Dominica. These islands too were full of fascination. They are each about twice the size of the Isle of Wight and their populations are around 100,000. The Atlantic Ocean crashes against their coasts to the East and the Caribbean Sea laps their shores to the West. They have beautiful beaches with silver sand and nodding palm trees. Everywhere the vegetation is luxurious - one could almost put a seed in the ground, stand back and watch it grow. There were lots of banana plantations, coconut palms, coffee, cocoa and a vast variety of fruits. Dominica has two specialities of its own - bay leaves and limes. Sugar cultivation has ceased in both islands - the difficulties of the terrain have made them uncompetitive. The southern part of Trinidad retains a large sugar industry, however, though it now has to struggle on world markets without its former protected access into Britain.

Life is a lot simpler in "the islands" than in Trinidad and the people's standard of living on the whole lower. As I moved from village to village and especially as I visited relatives of people in South London, I marvelled at the extraordinary contrast between the simple relaxed life of rural St Lucia and Dominica and the frantic complex existence that Caribbean people somehow adapted to in Britain. I was often told that when West Indians first started coming to Britain just after the Second World War, most thought that they would stay for perhaps five years, make a little money and then return home. It proved to be a long five years for most of them, but the dream of returning on retirement has stayed with a very large number of West Indian-born people and from the late nineteen-eighties onwards it had become a reality for many.

Two rural encounters emphasised the simplicity of life in the islands. I had promised to find the mother of a St Lucian who lived in Peckham. She told me her mother lived in a little place called Fond St Jacques which proved to be in the back of beyond near the town of Soufriere in the south of the island. I had been warned that the elderly lady spoke only patois so I was taken to her little cabin near the edge of the bush by the school teacher who interpreted for me. After she had been told who I was I had a battery of questions about her daughter and all her family. It was clear that the old lady had not the ghost of an idea about their life in London. I could have been describing life on Mars. Before I left I brought out my tape recorder and took her message. At first she spoke into the microphone expecting her daughter to answer as if it was a telephone but careful explanations from the schoolteacher eventually helped her to speak a little message in patois. When I got back to London and played the message over to her daughter, the tears rolled down her cheeks. The next summer she was able to go home and see her mother just a few months before she died.

The other encounter took place in Dominica. I was staying with one of the French priests in the village of Wesley and it was the season of Lent. The nearby village of Woodford Hill, a former sugar estate now growing bananas, was having a special week of prayer. In the village church-cum-hall all the community - the elderly, the dads and mums, the young people and the children, crowded in each evening. We sang, we prayed, I had to give a talk each time, all ages queued up to offer prayers of their own. Of course, with no television or other distractions, the evening prayers were the event of the week and the people entered into them with tremendous enthusiasm. When they came to an end and I was due to leave the island, I was surrounded by the people pressing gifts upon me. Lots gave me five Eastern Caribbean dollar bills worth about a pound at that time. I also received armfuls of produce including several breadfruits half as large as my head, mangoes and pawpaws. Dominica is the poorest of the English-speaking islands and Woodford Hill was among the poorest of its villages. Yet the people were rich in their affections and generosity.

Dominica had had a bad outbreak of Black Power violence a year before my visit. It seemed that the influence had come down from the United States brought by young fellows of middle class families who had gone to college there. Their anger against the status quo was aggravated by drug taking. Several visiting white people were shot and even some Irish Christian Brothers who ran St Mary's Academy, the most prestigious school in the island, felt under threat. For a short time near-anarchy reigned and the Prime Minister let it be known that proceedings would not be taken against anyone who shot an intruder on their property. By the time I reached the island, the crisis had passed and the young man who was thought to be the ring leader was in gaol. He languished there for some years without trial and was eventually released on appeal to the Privy Council. By then the danger had passed.

My personal impressions of the West Indies and my appreciation of black people and their struggles in relation to white society were greatly enlarged during my visit by the reading I did, mainly on my bed at siesta time. I read brief histories of each of the islands I was in and I read with fascination a history of the whole of the Caribbean by Sir Philip Sherlock of the University of the West Indies. Among the startling facts I learned there was that during the Anglo-French wars of the eighteenth century, Britain had contemplated trading the whole of eastern Canada for Martinique and Guadaloupe. These were days when Canada was a vast wilderness inhabited only by French people along the St Lawrence seaway, and Martinique and Guadaloupe were two valuable sugar islands in the Eastern Caribbean when sugar was the great international commodity - what oil is to-day.

The other weighty book I read was the *Autobiography of Malcolm X* ghosted by Alex Haley, author of *Roots*. Malcolm X was a powerful black activist in the United States in the sixties and seventies. His story was a chilling account of radical race politics of a kind that we had just a hint of in our brief brush with American Black Power activists in Brixton. Malcolm X became a Black Muslim in the United States and came to a violent end within that movement. He was not an endearing character but I did glean from the book a sense of the wounds in the soul that Black people have and that some of them feel acutely. Later, this was to help me understand a little of the cult of Rastafari which I was encountering in London and would see more of in Jamaica during my second visit to the West Indies in 1981.

I learned a vast amount from my first Caribbean visit. I began to appreciate our people in London in a new way, a more inward way. But I also came to realise my limitations. While I was in St Lucia, I went with one of the St Lucian priests to his Sunday morning Mass in a remote country village. He preached in patois and I marvelled at the electric communication that took place. Priest and people met somewhere in the air. It wasn't just the language, it was the sharing of a psyche, a culture and an experience of life. I reflected ruefully afterwards that there will be large areas of our people's minds and hearts that I will never be able to touch. I discussed this with one of the French priests and he said, "ah yes, but love is capable of speaking all languages". I was also encouraged by the example of Father Charles de Foucauld who spent a large part of his life alone among the Taureg people of the Sahara desert. One of his great dictums was, "identification is the measure of love". After eighteen years as chaplain to the black community in South London, I begin to understand what these good French priests meant.

Felix Henry with the name board which he designed and carved for the fifth anniversary of the opening of John Archer House.

*Ricky Mayers, for a long time leader of the "Bridges" choir,
entertaining members of the community at John Archer House.*

John Archer House

I moved into 135 Nightingale Lane at Balham early in December, 1977. It was a six-bedroom semi-detached house with a manageable garden front and back, manageable that is for someone with reasonable interest, skills and time to devote to it. The Holy Family sisters had left enough furniture to make the house habitable. I moved in the few things I had, notably my books which had been stored by some other kind sisters for the previous four years. The garage of the house had been converted by the Holy Family sisters into a chapel. They were happy to know that it would still be used as such after they had left. Small though it is, the chapel has been a precious feature of the house all the way through and it has accommodated a number of remarkable events. On several occasions, bishops visiting from the West Indies have celebrated Mass with the choir stacked up on the staircase outside and the congregation spilling over into the passageway and the front porch. The Archbishop of our Diocese came to lead other celebrations with similar cheerful exigences.

Marjorie Redhead

For a short time, I had Sister Phyllis Niles, a Trinidadian belonging to the Corpus Christi Carmelite order, working with me but sadly she fell ill shortly after beginning and had to resign. Charles Gaillard came to live at the house for some months while he was looking for a lodging in Peckham but otherwise I lived there on my own for the first nine months. During my stay in Trinidad in 1975 I had met two ladies who told me about their sister who was nursing in South London. This was Marjorie Redhead. It was a happy day for me and for the chaplaincy when I duly went to see her. She was working at the South London Hospital for Women at Clapham Common and lived in a small flat nearby. When we opened

135 Nightingale Lane she was a near neighbour. Some other Trinidadian friends came to stay during the summer of 1978, and while they were with me we asked Marjorie to come and spend an evening with us. The entail of this evening was that Marjorie gave up her flat and came to live at 135 as housekeeper.

It was a very considerable act of faith on her part. She scarcely knew me and in giving up the security of her own home, she had a great deal to lose. The financial advantage was marginal because all the time she continued to work at the hospital she contributed to the running costs of the house. The clinching factor was the good she could do for the Church and for her people. For the next eight years, Marjorie was at least half the heart of the chaplaincy. As time went on, nearly as many people came to the house to see her as me. There will be more to say about Marjorie before this story is finished.

The name "chaplaincy" was a convenient way of describing the ministry that I was engaged in; now it also designated the House - 135 Nightingale Lane - which came to be called "the Chaplaincy". Later on, we took the name "John Archer House". The reason for this is a story in itself and will be duly related. Installed in the house with Marjorie looking after the domesticities and much else besides, and having completed my engagement with the YCW, I was now able to give all my thoughts and energy to the work of the chaplaincy.

"Bridges"

I have described how we celebrated St Lucy's Day at our cathedral in December, 1977. We had always "ad hoc-ed" a choir for this event but challenged by the solemnity of having it at the cathedral, we enlarged the number of voices and had several practices. We also incorporated a good deal of the Caribbean music I had learned in Trinidad and some that we had developed ourselves. All this was duplicated up into a special service booklet in which we took some pride. At this time and for several years afterwards, Ricky Mayers was master of our music and choir leader. Ricky was in his late twenties at this time. He was born in Barbados and I had conducted his marriage some years before to Christiane, a French girl. They had two delightful children, Lisa and Roderick, who were both in the choir and the associated activities which developed.

St Lucy's Day, 1977, was the birth date of "Bridges". From then on we constituted the choir in a permanent form and added cultural activities to its singing. In these early days, Bridges was a marvellous amalgamation of mums and daughters and a few sons led by Ricky with his guitar and some other occasional instrumentalists. Altogether, we mustered around forty people - about ten adult women, three young boys and the rest young girls roughly between the ages of eight and eighteen. Most of them lived in the Peckham/East Dulwich area but every Sunday afternoon they made the considerable journey to the chaplaincy for the weekly practice.

Ricky had the ideas for developing the scope of the group. Early on, the girls - so we always called them even though some were boys and others were mums - discussed what name they would like to be known by. One of the younger ones - a girl called Anne - quietly suggested "Bridges" because, she said, "we want to build bridges between the races". Everybody else agreed enthusiastically and so "Bridges" it was and has remained.

"Tambourier" evokes the memories of Bridges early days. Ricky signed up a lady from Guyana who was a Caribbean adviser at the Commonwealth Institute and a skilled teacher of Caribbean song and dance. Her name was Doris Harper-Wills. She taught the girls a number of traditional group dances of which "Tambourier" - "Tambourine Player" - became their signature item. Doris had a marvellous sense of theatre and could even instil this into the girls as they danced in bare feet on the back lawn of 135 Nightingale Lane. A degree of fame came quickly. Bridges sang a Caribbean hymn "Wake up my People" in a television concert of modern church song. Shortly after this, they took part in a big Festival of London event at St Martin-in-the-Fields. They wore the national dress of the Eastern Caribbean with multi-coloured skirts, scarves and head-ties and looked quite gorgeous. And they made a tremendous hit with "Tambourier" and their other numbers.

These were two early high spots. They were also top billing at the celebrations of St Lucia's Independence at the Commonwealth Institute in February, 1979, this time accompanied by steel band music. Their regular engagements, however, were a programme of parish visits in South London and beyond. I would generally prompt an invitation from one of our parishes, most often in a multi-racial area, and Bridges would sing a Sunday Mass in the idiom of the Caribbean. By this time Bridges had also acquired a choir uniform of brown skirts and waistcoats with beige blouses and they were striking to the eye as well as to the ear. The mainly white congregations were captivated by both the vitality and worshipfulness of the girls singing. This was further evidence that the Caribbean gift for worship was as welcome to white congregations as to black. When the Mass was over (and as long as no other Mass was following) Bridges would generally add a few extra items. Always a considerable section of the congregation would linger behind to listen or sing with them. And - remarkable to say - the Mass seldom ended without a spontaneous round of applause.

"Cariba Steel"

In the summer of 1978, we managed to launch our steel band. We had the boys who were keen to start but we had no instruments and no teacher. The key development of 1978 was that Selwyn McSween swam into our orbit. Selwyn was another contact of Ricky Mayers. He hailed from Trinidad and had played with the "Desperados", one of the leading steel bands there. Selwyn was a research student working on a PhD in Caribbean economic history for a Canadian university. A loan from a friend of mine paid for a basic set of "pans" and a drumset and the Notre-Dame sisters who occupied one of the select houses on Clapham Common gave us the Sunday afternoon use of their garage. At the beginning, Selwyn lived at Dalston in North London and I had to go and pick him up every Sunday. Later he moved in at the chaplaincy and was able to do some evening sessions with the boys as well as Sundays. The lads made very rapid progress and soon one of them was able to understudy Selwyn as an arranger. Before long, they were earning money. Within eighteen months they had paid back the loan for the pans and had added to them. Eventually they had a bank of six tenor pans - these had the full notation scale and played the tune; two sets of basses - being five full drums giving a deep accompaniment; and two sets of seconds or "guitars" which gave an intermediate resonance. A complete steel band would duplicate or even triplicate each of these and add a few other tones. But our band in full cry made a sound that was exhilarating enough.

One of their early successes was a steel band version of "gaudeamus igitur"; later Stevie Wonder's "I just called to say I love you" was their show stopper. Selwyn had to leave us to go to Canada to present his thesis after about eighteen months, thereafter the lads did all their own arranging of tunes and all the training of fresh recruits. John Bonaparte became their manager and their engagements increased steadily. They were in demand for dances, private parties, official functions and often they joined Bridges for parish visits and other Church events, including an ordination. The name they chose for themselves was "Cariba Steel" - this was emblazoned on the pans. They were also arrayed in smart shirts made by the mother of one of them but I could never persuade them to go in for matching trousers. This eventually became a redundant idea because the band expanded into the feminine gender when no less than four sisters joined their big brother. The high spot of the year was the Notting Hill Carnival when the band would play from the back of a great Ford truck followed by troops of cavorting dancers, quite a few Bridges members among them.

This is a convenient point to describe the London carnival. The main inspiration comes from Trinidad as we have seen but most of the other Eastern Caribbean islands have Carnival too, though at different times in the year. It began in the Notting Hill area in the early sixties and for several years was a small local event always held on the summer bank holiday weekend in late August. Gradually it gathered momentum: more steel bands were formed and carnival costumes became more and more ambitious. And the crowds came. By the late seventies it had become one of the great London events of the year with hundreds of thousands of people on the streets, at least as many of them white as black. It had also become a public order problem. It occasioned a lot of street crime and confrontations between black youth and the police could easily break out.

Carnival

The first time I took part in the Carnival was in 1974. I joined a Dominican costume band with a number of my South West London friends. We met at Westbourne Park underground station, the womenfolk in national dress looking very colourful and the men in white frilly shirts with coloured sashes and straw hats. Our music duly appeared - a brass and drum ensemble mounted on the back of a Hammersmith municipal truck. We formed up behind the truck, the band struck up and we began to girate to the tune of "sukuya" (a witch!). At first we had the streets virtually to ourselves but as we got nearer to Ladbroke Grove and the centre of the action, hundreds of people of all races took the hospitality of our music and eventually the originals were just a few decorated heads bobbing up and down in a sea of undifferentiated revellers. By lunchtime "sukuya" was engraved on my memory forever. Our band did play one or two other tunes but it kept coming back to "sukuya". I hadn't taken in the fact that the band plays continuously and everybody has to keep moving. By the end of the day I had perfected a personal version of the "carnival shuffle", an economical movement which husbands one's energy until the next bout of serious dancing.

All was going very well until we got a few streets away from Ladbroke Grove. Rumours started flying of trouble there and then our truck broke down. The band kept playing because we had hundreds of people with us but we were tied to the same spot. Then suddenly bottles started flying. We had about a dozen policemen with us who dived into the source of the trouble but it soon became clear that our little set-to was a sideshow to a much bigger contest that was raging in Ladbroke Grove. The police were novices at handling public disorder on this scale at that time. They had no riot gear and very little training. There was a stabbing that day but apart from that there were no serious casualties. There was, however, a lot of mugging. Sadly, a day that began in high spirits ended up in fear and anger. Our group made its way back to Westbourne Park by back streets and we were glad to get home.

1974 proved to be the worst year of carnival disorder. Thereafter the police studied the technique of handling the crowds, the narrow streets and the street crime opportunities. Senior officers even went out to Trinidad to learn carnival policing but found the problems there different and much smaller. There was a lot of talk about confining the Carnival to a public park; some local residents wanted it banned altogether. Mercifully, no drastic negative action was taken. Carnival organisation gradually improved - though in truth, carnival and organisation are really a contradiction in terms. But the police, the borough representatives and members of the ad hoc carnival committees conferred in advance and succeeded in giving the event a little more shape and form. For some years afterwards there were sporadic outbreaks of disorder and there is still a lot of crime but these uglinesses gradually became drowned in an ever increasing ocean of people and ever increasing number of music bands and costume bands, by no means all of them composed of Caribbean people. And artistic standards are rising all the time. Today, the annual Notting Hill carnival is a splendid part of the London scene. It is a poor year if it doesn't attract half a million revellers. Other cities in Europe and North America with significant Caribbean populations have also blossomed into Carnival but none of them rivals London.

In the West Indies, the Church keeps herself aloof from Carnival because of its saturnalian underside. In London the churches affirm it. For one thing, Carnival is the event of the year when the whole nation focuses on the Caribbean community and it is clearly a gift of black people to the country as a whole. Also at Carnival time very many people are learning to appreciate and share West Indian culture. So it is very worth while for the churches to sacralise it. In the Catholic reckoning, there is always a great carnival Mass at St Mary of the Angels, Moorhouse Road, on the Saturday evening of the carnival weekend. Father Michael Hollings, the parish priest, is the impresario of the celebration. The Church is always packed to the doors. There is always a special motif in the decoration of the Church - one year it was "clowns of God" - and the Mass is tremendously vibrant. Afterwards, there is likely to be a steel band playing in the street outside and there is food and drink for all comers. Father Michael has long been recognised as "chaplain to the carnival".

A Christian way with money

February, 1979 saw the launch of the Credit Union. I had heard about this movement from several directions and I went to visit a branch at Camberwell. It met in the crypt of an Anglican church and during the evening a steady stream of people, black and white, called in to pay their dues, some to negotiate loans, others to take part in an informal discussion of Credit Union principles and all of them to socialise. I was enormously impressed by the good feeling of all the proceedings, the relaxed but efficient way that business was conducted and the evident democracy of it all - this was a dignified co-operative, run for the members by the members. It struck me too as a marvellously Christian way with money - it makes money do its proper job which is to facilitate the satisfaction of human needs.

Most people have to live to the limit of their incomes so that an unexpected expense like a funeral or a major outlay like kitting out children for a new school is an overstretch of their resources. For those who have established credit worthiness by regular saving these problems are solved by cheap loans, far lower in interest than bank loans or credit cards and miniscule in relation to the terms of money lenders. Moreover, borrowers pay interest only on the money they still owe. There is a little gentle scrutiny of a loan so that imprudent spending can be discouraged but in practice members are seldom refused for improvidence. They have to be refused if their loan request is out of proportion to their savings. All Credit Union branches must have a "common bond", that is a criterion of association which minimises the risk of bad faith.

The Camberwell common bond was a geographical one - every member had to live within a certain area of the Borough of Southwark. In the anonymity of a city like London this was a slightly risky one and I think they did have a higher than average "delinquency" rate. Nevertheless, it was clearly doing an excellent job for the great bulk of its members. The chairperson at the time of my enquiry was a Jamaican lady. She and her associates were more than ready to help us get going.

Our first attempt at a launch did not come off. We had the encouragement of the Camberwell team and we had three Sunday visits from the then Director of the Credit Union League of Great Britain, Mr Len Nuttall, who used to leave us about 9pm to drive home to Skelmersdale in Lancashire. There was no doubt that he believed in Credit Union with all his heart, indeed, he was a Credit Union evangelist. My South East friends did not take to the idea but when I got together a group of people in South West London there was a willingness to make a start. It was true that some of these had experienced the movement back home in the West Indies.

So we got going. We had just enough people to form our "board of directors", our "loans committee" and our "supervisory committee". The first was responsible for the management of our branch, the second adjudicated on the loans and the third had access to the books at all times to make sure that the management committee was doing its job honestly and efficiently. We chose as our common bond some sort of belonging in the chaplaincy - our members did not need to be black or Catholics (though most of them were both) but they had to relate to our community in some way. Later we were joined by a multi-racial (but mostly Irish) group in one of the Brixton parishes. Its members were happy to conform to our common bond and complete harmony has always reigned.

Our membership grew steadily but not overwhelmingly. It was always a regret with us that more people could not appreciate the benefits of Credit Union. After a couple of years we gained the reputation of being one of the best run branches in London. We were very fortunate in the commitment of our key people. A big part of our success was the dedication of our Treasurer, Marjorie Redhead. This role requires very considerable time and care and a Credit Union branch is empowered to pay its Treasurer an honorarium or, in the case of a big branch, a salary. Marjorie would not accept any recompense. Financially, our branch has prospered in a big way. We have a lot of money in reserve though we would far rather see it out on loans to our members. Our first loans limit was £50; we are now able to lend our members up to £1,000. In terms of practical benefit, Credit Union loans have helped one of our members to visit her family in the West Indies for the first time in years, another to go home for a family funeral; another had help to buy a house and yet another had the means of sustaining his small business. And we have had very little delinquency. Our branch also has a social life - always a Mass and Christmas party in December and on one famous occasion a "booze cruise" to Boulogne to lay in Christmas supplies.

Multi-racial development

In May, 1980, the Catholic community of England and Wales held its first National Pastoral Congress in Liverpool. Archbishop Derek Worlock of Liverpool is credited with the idea. It was certainly a new departure. For the first time, representatives of the whole Catholic community would deliberate together - bishops, priests, sisters, brothers, but the overwhelming majority would be lay people nominated by each of the dioceses according to their total Catholic populations. Our diocese - Southwark - being in the top middle range in numbers was allocated 147 places. This included our Archbishop and our three auxiliary bishops, a number of priests and sisters who had a special contribution to make and the rest were lay people. Among the latter was a large group of young people. When the diocesan preparations began, I made a special plea that ethnic communities should be represented. I did some bargaining with the diocesan organiser and eventually won eight special places - six Caribbean Catholics and two Asians. We also had two Caribbean youngsters, a boy and a girl, in the youth delegation and several others of our people were chosen by their local Catholic communities. Nevertheless we all prepared together.

The programme for the Congress was very wide ranging. There were broad categories of concern like Family, Social Welfare, Education, Justice and Peace together with more Church-centred categories like Liturgy and Catechises. All of these had topic sub-divisions - racial justice was part of the Justice and Peace category. The central preparations were very carefully laid and at the Congress itself the organisation was virtually impeccable. A total of three thousand people were accommodated, moved day by day to a large number of different locations and gathered together at the end for a huge plenary session and a memorable Mass in the cathedral.

For a year in advance of the Congress, our ethnic group held monthly meetings at the chaplaincy on Sunday afternoons. We prepared several submissions which we fed through to the central secretariat for inclusion on the agenda of the various topic headings. Our purpose was to make sure that the ethnic dimensions of all the topics should not go by default. Some of our group chose the racial justice topic but three of our number spread themselves between Family, Education and Liturgy. Both our advance thoughts for the preparations and our contributions at the Congress itself had considerable influence. We all felt that, small a group as we were, we had made an impact.

In addition, we brought another ethnic contribution to the Congress. The secretariat welcomed the idea of our bringing Bridges and Cariba Steel to present a special "Caribbean Mass" in Liverpool cathedral. This was an optional extra for the Congress delegates and took place on the Sunday afternoon. However, many delegates came and a number of others too who were in Liverpool for the Congress. Our normal amplification was augmented by the De La Salle brothers who took a great interest in our endeavours and band and choir made a splendid sound in the vast interior of the cathedral. Later that evening the steel band put on a special concert for the youth delegates and made another big impression.

For all who took part in it, the Congress was an exhilarating experience. Bishops sat down with lay people in discussion groups and listened! Somehow the work of each of the categories and topics was put together into coherent form for the plenary session which took place in the Liverpool concert hall. There were some radical proposals like modifications of the Church's contraception discipline and ecumenical guidelines but given the freedom of expression and the very wide spectrum of experience and opinion there was really a very remarkable harmony of heart and mind. The final Mass was unforgettable - all three thousand of us moved into the cathedral like an army with banners. The Mass expressed the missionary imperative of the Gospel - we were a people with a message and a purpose.

Following the Congress weekend, the bishops in council responded with a review of all the proceedings in a booklet *Easter People*. It was a good response reflecting the enthusiasm of event itself. Some of the revisionist features of the Congress were gently discouraged but there was no decisive embrace of any of the proposals that came forth. The Congress had happened - it was great, but now we have to get back to normal! Is it ever possible to translate an enthusiastic experience into a programme of action? Without some mechanism for implementation it could clearly be foreseen that the enthusiasm of the Congress would quickly run into the ground. And so it was.

Congress Continuation Group

However, when we got back from Liverpool, our Caribbean and Asian group decided that we would go on meeting and go on studying and campaigning for racial justice. So we turned ourselves into the "Congress Continuation Group for Multi-Racial Development" and with some of the originals and a number of newcomers, we have been active ever since.

Our first chairman, a member of our Liverpool delegation, was a Goan barrister, Mr Tony Lobo, who subsequently became the chairman of the Catholic Association for Racial Justice (CARJ), a national body which took on the mantle of the Catholic Commission for Racial Justice (CCRJ) when the bishops reorganised their commissions in 1984. The Congress

Group (later we dropped the word "continuation") gradually evolved a pattern of events. We organised an annual study weekend which attracted up to forty people. We also held a study day each Autumn with slightly less. We recruited participants for our weekends with the help of a number of parishes who would generally pay the expenses. Their object was to increase awareness in our parishes about multi-racial issues and to build up a body of support for multi-racial development. We ran a succession of excellent weekends and study days. Among the topics we dealt with were black people and the police, the effectiveness of the education system for black youth, the welfare of the black elderly, mental health in the black community and the most recent one, how black people would fare in post-1992 Europe.

We also conducted several campaigns. One was to encourage black people to register for citizenship, another was to urge the government to lower the costs of registration. The first succeeded very well; the second helped to shame the government to reduce the cost of straight-forward registration from £70 to £60 but they put it back up again later. I presented the Home Secretary with the case of one of our mothers who returned to the West Indies while pregnant with her third child and stayed for several years. The child was made in England though born in the West Indies. When she brought him back to Britain he had no automatic right to British citizenship not having been born here. Eventually it cost £200 to gain citizenship for him - this was the charge for naturalisation or "discretionary registration". The Home Office meanly refused any concession.

The first Brixton riots occurred in April, 1981. Everyone was dismayed by the extent and the fury of them. We were familiar with that sort of disorder in Northern Ireland but not in the cities of mainland Britain. It was now clear to everybody through the gruesome coverage on television that Britain had a racial problem. Lord Scarman was appointed quickly to enquire into the events leading up to the disorders

66

and to examine the underlying causes of them. He began by hearing submissions in sessions held at Church House, Westminster, then he moved his enquiries to Lambeth Town Hall. But he did not confine himself to those who came to see him. Remarkably for such an elderly gentleman, and for one embedded in the upper ranks of the establishment. he went out and about in the streets and meeting places of Lambeth Borough and exposed himself to the feelings and opinions of ordinary people.

Our Congress Group made a submission about the underlying causes of the disturbances and invited him to meet us and also a group of our young people. He agreed to come to the chaplaincy with Lady Scarman and his Secretary. On the day appointed, he first spent an hour and a half with the Congress members and afterwards another hour and a half with our youngsters. The adults made a favourable impression and put over some good points, most of which, however, he had by that time come alive to. It was the young people that made the greater impact. There were three boys and three girls, all around the age of eighteen. They had been meeting for over a year as a YCW group and had learned the basics of sensible thinking and coherent expression. Lord Scarman's previous experience of dialogue with black youth had been of passionate and confused assertions. The discussion was managed by one of the boys; one of the girls respectfully but firmly contradicted a statement of Lord Scarman's. Real communication took place and it was clear that the boys and girls had added a dimension to his thinking.

The result was that we were given a page and a bit in the report and I was invited to take part in the preparations for the launching of the Community/Police Consultative Group for Lambeth in March, 1982. The formation of the Consultative Group was the first fruits of Lord Scarman's report which was published in December of 1981. When the prospect of my being involved arose, the Congress Group was full of encouragement. This sort of involvement in a race issue of major importance was absolutely in line with our purpose as a Group. It would possibly have been better if the job had fallen to one of our lay black or Asian members but none of them at that time were near enough to the Lambeth scene. There is a lot more to say about the Brixton upheaval and its aftermath. It is simply worth noting here that the Congress Group constituted a means by which black and Asian Catholics could react to the problem posed by the riots.

Mother and daughters in national dress, members of the "Bridges" Choir and Dance Group at the Festival of London at St Martins-in- the-fields.

"Bridges" members with their manager, Charles Gaillard (left) who was ordained priest in September 1993 and John Bonaparte (right) who managed the steel band, and is now a deacon.

Bishop John Jukes with "Bridges" members in their choir uniform at an Aylesford pilgrimage.

Second Caribbean visit

"Caribbean Catholic"

In October, 1979, the first edition of "Caribbean Catholic" appeared. We had long needed a newsletter to notify our people about events and projects. As the issues succeeded one another, however, we found that it was doing a great deal to raise our people's sense of themselves as black Catholics and to win us understanding and sympathy in the Catholic community as a whole. To begin with, Mable Thompson, a senior civil servant who had been a journalist in Guyana, was my co-editor and typist. We planned "Caribbean Catholic" together and met regularly to prepare the monthly issues. The ingredients were "news from home" - most months we carried a news story from somewhere in the Caribbean; "West Indians in London" - a feature about our people's experience here; "People, Places and Events" - a lot of human interest notes and records of occasions like weddings, baptisms and exam successes; "Prayers" - for our sick people and for those who had died. Each issue concluded with a footnote by me - some little spiritual message which, however brief, often took me a long time to write.

Each monthly issue encompassed two sides of a single sheet of paper. At first we used foolscap and later A4. Our title, chaplaincy derivation and address was printed at the top in red. Issue number 1 of October 1979 was published at 2p and circulated 400 copies, some through friendly parishes but most through a network of individual distributors. We rapidly built this up largely by drawing in an ever increasing number of parish outlets. We eventually had over fifty parish distributors all of whom would pay for a year's supply in advance. Some batches we sent by post but most were delivered by a devoted team of drivers who each gave their time and petrol. We also developed a considerable postal distribution to friends and supporters. Most of the bishops in the West Indies were on our mailing list in addition to our own Archbishop and auxiliary bishops. All the Catholic papers were subscribers and would often reproduce our material and we exchanged with "Alizes" ("Trade Winds"), the (much more ambitious than us) magazine of the French Caribbean chaplaincy in Paris. At the end, after over twelve years of publication and 147 issues we were circulating 1,200 copies each month at 10p a copy.

One of our notable successes concerned a story that we printed about a Guyanese child, Anastasia, who was brought to London by her mother for treatment of a heart condition at the childrens' hospital at Great Ormond Street. The child had no claim on the National Health Service in Britain, Guyana being an independent country though in the Commonwealth, so money had to be found to pay for her treatment. Our story in "Caribbean Catholic" was reproduced in *The Universe* and *The Catholic Herald* and money came in from all over Britain and Ireland. Eventually we were sent over £5,000, enough to pay for investigations at Great Ormond Street, a pilgrimage to Lourdes for the child and her mother and airfares back to Guyana. Sadly, the doctors found that they could not operate on Anastasia but prescribed physio-therapy and drug treatment and this and Lourdes have managed to preserve her life beyond all expectations. The fund is still paying for the drugs she needs.

Second West Indies visit

In January, 1981, I made my second visit to the Caribbean. This time I went first to Jamaica via Bermuda. I was astonished that Bermuda is so far out in the Atlantic from the North American seaboard. None of the island group seems more than fifty feet above sea level and they all looked lonely and vulnerable in that huge expanse of ocean.

In Kingston, Jamaica, I was the guest of the Jesuits of the Boston (USA) Province who ran St George's College, one of the most prestigious schools in the island. They were also in charge of the cathedral and numerous parishes. Most of the Jesuit fathers were Americans but several are native Jamaicans, including the Archbishop, Monsignor Sam Carter. The Catholics in Jamaica are no more than 10% of the population but the Church is influential beyond its numbers in an island which respects religion. Shortly after I arrived, Archbishop Carter presided over a "prayer breakfast" with the prime minister and the leader of the opposition on either side of him.

Just a few months before, Jamaica had been almost split apart by a general election campaign which had cost dozens of lives. No one can deny the fact that Jamaica is a violent country. This is especially true in down-town Kingston where politics, gangsterism and drug trafficking are closely intertwined. Both the main political parties, that of Mr Michael Manley and that of Mr Robert Seaga, had embarrassing friends. Kingston 8, the heartland of the city's deprivation and turbulence, was a patchwork of small localities each with a single and unchallenged political allegiance. It was impossible to live in one of these enclaves if you were thought to be not "one of us". Its Catholic parish of St Anne's (always known as "St Annie's") had a large notice pinned up by the sanctuary at the time of my visit listing the victims of the election campaign. There were over fifty entries ranging from "burned out" to "slain". The 1980 election went Mr Seaga's way but Mr Manley retained his personal popularity and he was eventually re-elected. Jamaican politics were complicated at that time by relations with Cuba. Mr Manley's government had enlisted the help of Fidel Castro in various development projects. The Cubans in Jamaica, however, behaved arrogantly and had meddled in Jamaican affairs. Mr Seaga's promise to get rid of them was enough to get him elected.

The gun laws were also an important issue in the early eighties. In an effort to contain gang murder and intimidation, a law had been enacted for detention without trial for anyone found with a gun. It may or may not have had the desired effect but one of the Jamaican Catholic priests, Canon Alwin Harry, carried out an unrelenting campaign against the principle of detention without trial. This won him a lot of friends among down-town Kingstonians (he was the parish priest of St Annie's at the time) and after several years he won.

It was very enlightening for me to see how far the Brixton scene in London was a reflection of Kingston 8. The colour, the vitality, the human kaleidoscope and the people's need and the heartbreak were all immediately recognisable. Later on in London we became supporters of Father Richard Ho Lung's Faith communities in Kingston. Father Richard had created the Little Brothers of the Poor to care for those in desperate poverty. Their centres survived a disastrous fire and in September, 1988, the devastation of Hurricane "Gilbert" which blew away a third of the island's dwellings and all the crops. In London we managed to raise over £9,000 to send to Archbishop Carter for hurricane relief by a general appeal to our parishes and this was despite the fact that appeals were being made for famine relief in Africa and Bangladesh at the same time.

During my visit to Jamaica, I came to understand the cult of Rastafari a little better. There was a big Rasta community at Buff Bay on the north coast and there seemed to be a great deal of Rasta-type influence in the university and in the world of the arts. The cult goes back to a visit paid to Jamaica by the Ethiopian Emperor, Haile Selassie, in the early 1930s. The idea grew that the Emperor represented an African civilisation that pre-dated the European and moreover had nothing to do with the slave coast of West Africa. By the nineteen-eighties, the cult had developed a dress, a form of speech and a whole set of customs and relationships of its own. The smoking of cannabis, "the holy weed", was an integral part of the cult and reggae was its characteristic form of music. Bob Marley and "The Wailers" were the arch-exponents of reggae and became internationally famous.

Perhaps no one has communicated the feeling of the Rasta cult and with it the broad sentiment of black people in general more than Bob Marley. His image in tam and dreadlocks gripping his electric guitar and pouring out his soul into a microphone is one of the unforgettable evocations of these times. And the music too cannot but last because it expresses such deeply felt experience. White people can only appreciate these things from a distance, but the effort to understand is in itself an act of affection and respect.

The cult of Rastafari - I learned that it was wrong to speak of "Rastafarians" as if the devotees were a movement or an organisation - is most significant, in my judgement, as the embodiment of a state of soul and as a quest for self discovery. It encompasses a whole range of feeling. At one end it is almost completely a pastoral ideal: natural food, natural relationships, all things in common, no truck with the artificialities of white civilisation and great respect for God understood as "JAH" of the Old Testament. At another point in the spectrum the cult can be very aggressive, very acquisitive and very corrupt. And there are many part-time Rastas - people who wear dreadlocks and a tam but otherwise take a part in general society. But in all degrees, the cult signifies belonging and identity. One of our young men was facing a serious court case and I murmured to him that he might stand a better chance with the judge and jury if he cut off his dreadlocks. He understood my good intentions but his identity as a person mattered more to him even than the possibility of lenient treatment in court.

My three weeks in Jamaica were full of other discoveries. I visited an old sugar estate in a secluded corner of the island called the Luidas Vale. It was Oliver Cromwell's men who took Jamaica off the Spaniards in 1655. Part of the Luidas Vale was awarded to Captain Price; the graves of his descendants can still be seen around the little Anglican church in the valley. I read a history of the estate, "Worthy Park", in advance of my visit - this was why I was keen to see it. Alas, parts of the story made shameful reading. The whole sorry story of slavery was there and also a vignette of the economic history of the island.

One of the priests took time off from his work to drive me almost completely round the island. We saw the beauties of the north and west coasts including Montego Bay, bauxite workings in the interior and in the savannah country, I was fascinated by the cattle, each one with its personal white egret bird in attendance. The office of the egret is to peck off the ticks from its big partner's hide; it seems to be an arrangement of perfect mutuality. I also sampled "jerk chicken" during my travels. This is a Jamaican speciality: jerk chicken or jerk pork is a form of barbecue; the secret lies both in the spices in which the meat is soaked beforehand and in the technique of the cooking. The origin of the dish is said to go back to pirate times.

From Jamaica, I flew on to the Eastern Caribbean, a five-hour flight across the Caribbean sea. I saw St Lucia and Dominica again and I was also in Trinidad for another Carnival, every bit as rich and enjoyable as the previous one - more so, really, because I now understood things better. But my Eastern Caribbean itinerary took in Grenada for the first time. Grenada was undergoing a mild revolution at this time under the leadership of Maurice Bishop who had replaced a regime only slightly less oppressive than that of Papa Doc's in Haiti. Maurice Bishop was popular with most Grenadians but, alas, he too made the mistake of bringing in the Cubans. When he was murdered by some of his more radical and unprincipled henchmen, the American marines moved in with the co-operation of the governments of some other English speaking islands.

When I was there, the most obvious signs of revolution were large slogan boards at the entrance of each village with such exhortations as "All students must work the land". There were also militia men with tommy guns hanging from their necks and wearing Fidel-type peaked fatigue caps. But these were counterbalanced by the Deputy Police Chief in resplendent British-type khaki drill and Sam Browne belt. This was "Lucky" Bernard whom I count it a great privilege to have known. He was a splendid looking man and had a marvellously open and cheerful personality. Two attempts had been made to assassinate him, he was quite incorruptible and simple people were always coming to him for advice. Besides being a top policeman, he was also a deacon in the Church and was at Mass every morning. He died a year or two after my visit. I do not know if it was a natural death or whether his enemies succeeded in killing him at their third attempt.

Another memorable feature of my visit to Grenada was a weekend trip to the island of Carriacou, one of the Grenadine islands to the north of Grenada proper. All my island hopping had previously been made by the Liat company's light aircraft but this trip I made by schooner. I had realised during my visit of 1975 that no experience of the Caribbean is complete without an island to island journey by sea. The voyage from St George's, the capital and seaport of Grenada, to Hillsborough in Carriacou took five hours. The front deck was piled high with cargo - baulks of timber, great stalks of bananas, crates of live chickens among the items. The passengers were equally diverse. It was a Saturday afternoon and there were secondary school youngsters going home for the weekend. One of the lads had a radio glued to his ear with a ball by ball commentary of a cricket match between Barbados and the Windward Islands. There was a large lady with a huge basket of fruit and ground provisions. A farmer from Devon in England was there with his wife. One of the crew members did a brisk trade in beers dispensed from a large tub filled with ice. Another of the crew had a fishing line out and hauled in a large king snapper amid great excitement. The motive power was a sail-assisted engine. Looking up at the sail and viewing the densely forested shore, one could easily imagine what some seventeenth century Caribbean landfall might have been like. Carriacou itself was also a Caribbean idyll. I sat that evening in the veranda of the priests' house with the water of the bay lapping in a few feet away sipping a rum and coke and watching the sun go down. The world felt like a very good place.

The New Cross tragedy

While I was away a great tragedy occurred at New Cross in South East London. Thirteen young people died in a house fire following an all-night party. Another died later from the traumatic effects of that terrible night. The tragedy happened on January 18th, 1981, and was big news in Jamaica while I was there. As soon as the news broke I rang home and discovered that one of the victims was a Bridges choir girl, Roselyn (or as we knew her, Lilian) Henry. Later the heart-breaking circumstance became known that Lilian had in fact got out of the house but she had gone back in to look for her boy friend. He, in fact, had managed to get out from the back. Poor Lilian never emerged again, her body was found huddled in a corner.

At roughly the same time there was a similar tragedy in Dublin with many more deaths. The Queen and Mrs Thatcher sent messages of sympathy. Unfortunately, no such message was offered to the black community of South London. There was also strong suspicion that the fire had been a racist attack. Something like an explosion was observed in one of the ground floor rooms and the fire spread with astonishing rapidity. These circumstances were enough to incense black people in South London and beyond. A large protest march was organised and violence broke out towards the end of it. "Thirteen dead, nothing said" was the cry. The white population of the area drew away, perhaps out of respect for the grief of black people, perhaps because they did not know how to articulate their sympathy. The inquest into the deaths of the young people was a very fraught proceeding and for months afterwards, black and white communities were polarised.

The situation was saved by the churches. Special care was taken over the funerals of each of the young people. The Catholic Archbishop visited the area and said a special Mass in the Catholic parish church. Other services were conducted by the Anglicans and Methodists and in the Pentecostal congregations. For ten years afterwards all the Christian communities came together for an annual memorial service. The early ones attracted huge gatherings of people with representatives of the Caribbean High Commissions and of the South London municipalities. We had several beautiful memorial masses for our Lilian with choir and steel band and what seemed to be a full turn out of our young people. The mood of these occasions changed with the years. At first they were full of indignation but they mellowed with the passage of time, though they never lost their poignancy. The whole experience showed how important it is for a community to be able to express and live out its anger and distress. The churches succeeded in helping the people with this while official Britain failed.

Five years on

On December 4th, 1982, we celebrated the fifth anniversary of the opening of 135 Nightingale Lane as our chaplaincy centre. The Archbishop came and celebrated Mass in our little chapel with a large gathering of our people overflowing into the hall and stairs, the back kitchen and on the porch outside. Marjorie Redhead with a team of helpers had prepared a small banquet which included a large birthday cake. We took the occasion for giving the house a name. It was now to be known as "John Archer House".

John Archer was the son of a Barbadian father and an Irish mother. He came to London from Liverpool towards the end of the last century to study medicine. He never got into the medical profession; instead he became a photographer in Battersea. What is more to the point, he became very involved in local politics and in 1913 he was elected mayor of the old borough of Battersea. His election was a national event - a "man of colour" had become the first citizen of a London borough and not without opposition. John Archer's acceptance speech was a prophetic foreshadowing of post Second World War London and a slightly ironical one. He said to the citizens of Battersea, "what you have done will ring round the world ... you have shown that you take no account of the colour of a man's skin but you look to what he has done". Alas, John Archer's election did not signify that the British working class were innocent of racism but it did give an indication that particular individuals could cause the white population to rise above racial prejudice and gain its support for public office. Happily, in the nineteen-eighties we began to see more and more instances of this.

John Archer was a very suitable patron for our house on four scores. First, he was a Catholic, always an observant one and one who expressed his faith in the service of the poor. Second, our house was located on the territory of his old mayoral borough. Third, he used to describe himself as a "Black Englishman" - he was convinced that his was a true belonging in Britain and this is something that our present black young people need to be persuaded about. And fourth, John Archer was a great "Pan-Africanist" - he worked ardently for the liberation of black people in all parts of the world, attending the early Pan-African congresses which campaigned for the de-colonisation of black Africa".

At our fifth anniversary party, Mr Chris Power, a former history teacher at Tulse Hill School who with a colleague had written a school book about notable black people in Britain, came and gave a splendid lecture on John Archer. One of our young men had carved a board with the words "John Archer House" - this was solemnly blessed by the Archbishop and ceremoniously hung in the porch. Marjorie received a fine bouquet of flowers and we celebrated far into the night.

Brixton riots and

the Consultative Group

Mention has been made of the bad relations in Lambeth between the Police and black youth and the efforts - mainly fruitless - of the Council for Community Relations (CCR) to sweeten them. From the Police point of view, the rising levels of crime, and especially street crime or muggings, were intolerable. Most of the public thought so too. In Lambeth street crime was perpetrated for the most part by black youth. I think it is undeniable that over a period the average police officer developed an apprehension growing into an antagonism towards black young people. While the "sus" law - a nineteenth century statute which gave police officers the right to stop and search people simply "on suspicion" - was widely used against young black lads and it became the symbol of their distrust and antagonism towards the Police. Stopping and searching was often accompanied - so the youngsters constantly avowed - by insults and abuse. The problem was compounded by the hostility of Lambeth Council towards the local Police. Councillors of the Labour majority party accused them of racism and refused all co-operation. "L" District (as then existed) of the Metropolitan Police felt ill-understood and ill-appreciated. The senior officers retired to their redoubts and surveyed the scene in almost complete isolation.

The eruption

This was the background to the launch of "operation swamp" by the Brixton Police in April, 1981. A large number of young plain clothes officers were drafted in and began a drastic programme of stop and search with mainly black lads at the receiving end. Tension steadily mounted. On the Friday evening of the Palm Sunday weekend, some uniformed policemen tried to search a car outside the "Front Line" mini cab office in Atlantic Road. In no time, a large crowd of black men converged on the scene and disorder broke out. There were running battles for the rest of that evening and no one could doubt that the stage was set for more trouble the following day. The surprise was the ferocity of it.

There is an anatomy to a riot. The first pre-requisite is an underlying feeling of anger and grievance. Then there needs to be factors which bring these feelings to the surface. Almost any incident can then trigger off the trouble. With disorder threatening the hard men move in and set about orchestrating it. Once the mayhem is under way all sorts of people join in, some of them for the excitement, others for the looting and other crimes.

The Brixton Police became convinced that the riots were the result of an anarchist conspiracy. I am not sure that they persuaded Lord Scarman, who subsequently produced his famous report, that this was so. There was, however, considerable evidence that hard men, including some white men, aggravated the trouble once it had broken out. It is likely that it was white activists who spread the idea of petrol bombs. The angry, the curious, the avaricious and the malign all moved into Brixton on the Saturday. There were also large numbers of Police drafted in and the battle duly began in the afternoon. The policemen and women had no riot gear. They were confronted by hails of missiles, some of them from very close range in the narrow streets and then came the petrol bombs. These forced the Police to retreat and it looked at one point as if all control might be lost. It is to the credit of ordinary police officers that on that day a thin blue line did hold. Lord Scarman duly commended them in his report. One policeman told me a long time afterwards that with his uniform alight that afternoon, a big black man bundled him over and beat out the flames with his hands. For one rioter at least, it may have been a furious battle but it was not unto death.

Nearly two hundred officers were injured that day and quite a lot of the rioters. But - and it is worth emphasising - no one was killed. Eruptions in American cities in the sixties and seventies had produced big death tolls. It is fair to conclude - a conclusion supported by other experience - that there was a limit to the anger directed against the Police. The black youngsters wanted to score a big "own back", they wanted to hurt but they did not - at least most of them - want to kill.

Fully occupied with the battle for the streets, the Police had to abandon the main shopping area. For perhaps five hours the looters had a free market. Many of these were white people and some came from a distance. The latter reacted quickly to the opportunity of the riot and came in with their shopping bags. Brixton was a sorry sight when order was finally restored.

There was some attempt to resume the battle on the Sunday but the trouble was sporadic and unsustained. Brixton could now lick its wounds and ruminate over the disaster that had struck it. The Home Secretary, William Whitelaw, was quickly on the scene. Our Archbishop came on the Tuesday; he visited the two Brixton Catholic parishes and toured the streets in the Front Line area. Television crews, needless to tell, had a field day but sometimes they had to beat a hasty retreat because media people are not popular in Brixton. They are believed to perpetuate too many negative images. There were indeed quite a few foreign journalists stalking the streets because the riots had engendered huge international interest. Railton Road became nearly as storied a thoroughfare as the Falls Road in Belfast.

Some black and white activists began to describe the riots as an "uprising". If "uprising" signifies black popular protest against racist attitudes in society at large and in the Police in particular then the term has some relevance. The protesters, of course, had no specific objective and no coherent message to communicate. The upheaval had to be "read" for the message to come through. This is precisely what all our commentators hastened to do. For a while, the focus of the nation was on Brixton and the black community and we began to learn one of the hard lessons of a multi-racial society. Apropos of the Brixton eruption, I later heard a thoughtful black person say, "Britain has three possibilities before her: one is that all the black, brown or yellow people will go 'home'; or they will stay and disturb the natives by clamouring for recognition and their rights; or we will make a success of a multi-racial society".

Of course, though for some it may have been genuinely an "uprising", for many more the upheaval was predominantly criminal. Looting, arson, knifings and rape have nothing to do with advancing the cause of black people in Britain. Unfortunately, many white people, especially those who lived a long way from inter-racial areas, having failed to learn to love black people, now began to fear them.

Lord Scarman reports and consultation begins

The shock had barely passed before Lord Scarman was appointed to enquire into riots. His first brief was to look into the events leading up to the disturbances. Very soon this was expanded to include the underlying causes. For those who did not know him, Lord Scarman was an unpromising choice. He was elderly, looked very like an establishment figure and seemed innocent of any particular knowledge of the black community. However, he proved to be an inspired choice. I have already described the various phases of his enquiries and how he responded to an invitation to meet members of our Congress and Young Christian Workers groups. Both groups had previously submitted written comments about the underlying causes.

The meetings took place in October of 1981 at John Archer House. Lord Scarman came with Lady Scarman and his civil service secretary, Mr Philip Mawer. He told us at the outset that we had got him at the formative time. He had already collected a vast amount of evidence and was about to embark on the writing of the report. During the discussions, it was possible to see when we were telling him things that he had already digested and when we were making some impression on his mind. As I have already said, it was the young people who impressed him most. The conversation centred on the problem of being both black and British. The boys and girls said very forthrightly that black youth had very little sense of belonging in Britain; indeed, they had plenty of reason to feel rejected. All the boys and some of the girls had stories of humiliations received from police officers. None of them had actually thrown anything at the Police during the riots but they all understood very well the feelings of those who had.

Lord Scarman's report was published in November of 1981. It proved to be a landmark in the development of race relations in Britain. It could fairly be said that for the first time, black people could feel that they had been understood in the higher counsels of the nation. The report was detailed and specific about what had gone wrong in Brixton and his recommendations were equally on the spot. With reference to the breakdown in Police and community relations in Brixton in the period before the riots, one of his key recommendations was that consultative mechanisms should be set up in all the London boroughs so that a continuous dialogue could take place between senior police officers and representatives of the community.

Launch of the Lambeth Consultative Group

Anxious perhaps to make an immediate response, the Home Office seized on this crucial recommendation and what better place to implement it than in Lambeth where the riots had occurred! Moreover, their first anniversary was approaching and there was a virtue in getting something in place within a year. Accordingly, Mr Whitelaw called a whole collection of people to the Home Office in January of 1982. I was invited - I think - on the strength of our discussions with Lord Scarman.

The top brass at Scotland Yard was there, also all four of the MPs that Lambeth had at the time, together with a considerable number of Borough and County councillors. In addition, there was a whole troop of "community leaders": representatives of the churches, the chambers of commerce, local trades councils, the Moslem community, the Rastafarians (more accurately to be described as devotees of Rastafari) and the Brixton Domino Club. Lord Scarman's proposal was examined in relation to the Lambeth scene. Most of us had a good deal of catching up to do so the discussion was inconclusive. A group of us were designated to sharpen up the proposal and there was a further meeting of all the original invitees with Mr Whitelaw to make the commitment to action. The inaugural meeting took place at Lambeth Town Hall on March 3rd, 1982. Mr Timothy Raison, a Minister of State at the Home Office presided.

Our first business was to choose a chairperson. It was agreed without argument that we wanted neither a policeman nor a politician. Several people were nominated and declined and then I was named and elected unanimously. Mr Raison withdrew and we got down to business straightaway. We quickly settled the terms of membership with the number of councillors, borough and county, with the right to vote, also the number of "statutory" seats like those allocated to policemen and representatives of such bodies as the Inner London Education Authority. In the process we established the very important principle that representatives of local voluntary organisations should outnumber all the rest. There was a distinct feeling of democracy in the air.

We were assisted at this first meeting by a set of proposals which had been prepared by the officers of the Council of Community Relations in concert with some members of the Brixton Council of Churches. Before we parted at that first meeting we reached a crucial accord with the Police. The officer in charge of the Lambeth Police, Commander Brian Fairbairn, agreed that he would always consult us in advance of any major operation except when the nature of the operation required secrecy, in which case he would always account to us afterwards. This commitment went way beyond the terms of any previous form of dialogue and was immensely confidence inspiring.

Open Forum

Early on, we also declared ourselves to be an open forum. Any citizen, we said, has a right to come to our meetings and at the discretion of the chair speak his or her mind. We elaborated this by stages. One evening, three black men came and indicated that they had a matter to raise. They waited patiently while we worked our way through the agenda until we came to "any other business". Given the floor, they brought to light a piece of malpractice by policemen which should have taken precedence over all the other business of the evening. Apparently, they had been made to drop their trousers in a public place for officers to make an "intimate" search for drugs. The Police Commander when pressed agreed that his officers had behaved improperly. This incident had two important effects. In the first place it guided our minds to ask for a very clear code of practice for officers conducting stops and searches and we contributed to this (and gained satisfaction) when we came to examine the "Police and Criminal Evidence Bill" in 1983/4.

The second lesson of the three men's intervention was that we must be ready to give immediate priority to such incidents as they had raised. Other less patient interventions had emphasised the point. So we created a category of business called "matters of immediate public importance" and these would take priority over any other items, even to the extent of jettisoning the whole agenda for an evening.

As soon as we had fixed our terms of reference and our finances, we gave our attention to a paper prepared by the Police Commander on the incidence of serious crime in the Borough. We were meeting twice each month in these early days, nevertheless, the Commander's paper took us months to get through. At first, there was a great deal of strident criticism of the Police. The Commander and his senior officers had to take a lot on the chin. Gradually, however, members of the Group began to appreciate what the Police were up against. The crime levels were excruciating and the Front Line district around Railton Road was virtually a "no-go area". Gradually we developed a sense of common cause with the Police. By this time the Commander was asking our advice about what to do. On one famous occasion, he asked us what should be his policy about the Railton Road area - if his officers tried to crack down on the crime there he could have another riot on his hands; if he did nothing, he surrendered the streets to lawlessness.

There had been a disposition on the part of some policemen - not the Commander - to engage in the consultative process simply because the Home Office and Scotland Yard wanted it. This request, however, was a challenge to the Group to articulate a public protest against crime and to play a part in combatting it.

A few of us were in a position to facilitate encounters with some of the "Front-Liners". The problem centred on a row of "shebeens" - 50, 52 and 54 Railton Road. These had become an open drug market and various other nefarious activities flourished there. Buses sometimes had a job to get through with the large numbers of habitués spilling over into the road and occasionally a bus conductor would lose his takings. Law abiding citizens took great care to avoid the locality. Indeed, we had a group of local residents - black and white - at one meeting demanding a "clean-up". The idea being canvassed was that the "shebeens" should be relocated and dispersed. This would recognise that they had a legitimate social value and at the same time reduce the lawlessness that coagulated around them.

Early on November 1st, 1982, Lambeth Council (briefly under Conservative administration) sent in men to demolish the three Railton Road houses. The Council owned them, they were being used for illegal drinking and the operators had been warned that they were to come down on November 1st. The operators had been warned but not the clientele. The Police laid on a low profile presence in protection of the workmen (they had many more men in reserve) and during the morning everything seemed to be going fairly smoothly. The Council had grasped the "Front Line" nettle and maybe they were not going to be stung. By lunchtime, however, the "Front-Liners" had woken up to the fact that their citadels were under attack. A large crowd gathered and a section of it headed for the Town Hall, attacking a black licensee known to be a supporter of law and order on the way. The streets seethed with indignation all that day and when dusk fell the riot duly broke out. This time though, the Police did have riot gear and they had greatly improved their tactics and the trouble was fairly easily contained.

The Group comes of age

The Consultative Group had one of its regular meetings the following evening. Word got around that the "Front-Liners" would be coming. In these early days the Group attracted a great deal of media attention; reporters from *The Times* and *The Guardian* attended every meeting. But this time it became known that the meeting would be especially lively and all Fleet Street was represented and there were at least three television crews. Sure enough, the Front-Liners turned up in force, some with their faces swathed in scarves. The agenda went out of the window straightaway and the irate questions began to flow. For once it was the Council and not the Police that came under the heaviest attack. Why weren't the habitués of the "Front-Line" warned about the demolitions? How many police officers were deployed? Why weren't they showing their police numerals on their riot overalls? Amazingly, some semblance of order was maintained; the important questions were recorded and action promised. Many of our members believe that the Group came of age that evening. The Consultative Group had really been recognised by a deeply alienated section of the community as the right forum for Police and community confrontation and that we had been able to absorb the shock of a major dispute.

This was not our only climacteric meeting. An even greater eruption took place during my successor's chairmanship. He was a very widely respected black youth worker; I was his vice-chairman. The occasion of this trouble was the accidental shooting at her home of Mrs Cherry Grose by police officers who were looking for her son wanted for robbery. Mrs Grose suffered permanent injury. This tragedy on September 28th, 1985, led to another weekend of violent disturbances. At the Group's meeting the following Tuesday a huge crowd turned up, necessitating a move into the main assembly room at Lambeth Town Hall. The threat of violence was very immediate but eventually, people queued up to use the microphone to denigrate the Police. A new head of Lambeth's Police, Commander Alex Murdoch, bore the brunt that evening and saved the day. He made no attempt to explain away the disaster and recognised the anger and distress of the community.

The Group was in despair following this second Brixton upheaval - the very thing we existed to prevent had happened again. We had an emergency meeting at the West Indian Ex-Servicemen's Club at Clapham. Some of our number were inclined to pull out but the reflection that prevailed was "what hope have the people got without us?". This victory of hope over despair was probably the second high spot in the life of the Group.

The Consultative Group consolidates

Fortunately not all our meetings were fraught. Some were very decorous, as when we gave detailed consideration in full session to the Police and Criminal Evidence Bill. We were led in this by a diminutive but redoubtable Quaker lady who subsequently became our third chairperson. During these deliberations, Mr Douglas Hurd, then another Minister of State at the Home Office, attended one of our meetings at Lambeth Town Hall. In his presence, we discussed the length of time a suspect could be held without charge. One of our members declared with great feeling that any extension of the statutory minimum must be sanctioned by a magistrate. Mr Hurd noted this and the point was duly incorporated into the bill. Our detailed discussions led to other modifications by the government. We were particularly keen, among other things, that stop and search procedures should be tightly controlled. This was accepted and so were our recommendations about the development of consultative groups like ourselves throughout the country.

The Group had other influential achievements. Lord Scarman in his report had noted that dark things were said about the treatment of suspects in police stations. He suggested that these suspicions might be allayed if police stations somehow came under public scrutiny. This was another of his creative ideas, witnessing to the depth of his understanding of Lambeth's problems. Again, it was the Quaker lady who got us down to brass tacks on this. After a great deal of debate and negotiation with the Home Office and Scotland Yard, our "Lay Visitors to Police Stations" project was launched.

The scheme provided for the recruitment of 24 members of the public - all would have to be vetted by the Home Office - who, after a little basic training, would be authorised to visit police stations at any time, night or day, without warning. The officer in charge of custody had to allow them to see any prisoner who wanted to see them. The visitors - they would always visit in pairs - could enquire into the basic welfare of suspects and hear any complaints they might have. They were not allowed to get involved with a suspect's case. If they found anything amiss they could make immediate representations to the custody officer and to the officer in charge of the station. In addition, there were regular meetings of the Lay Visitors Panel, which were always attended by a senior officer of the Lambeth Police, at which particular problems and matters of general concern could be aired. The Panel reported regularly to the Home Office (to which it had direct access) and twice-yearly to the Consultative Group. The latter administered the Panel and handled its recruitment but otherwise it was autonomous.

The Lay Visitors scheme was highly imaginative, it attracted for its members a very wide cross section of the Lambeth community, and it quickly began to have an effect. In the first place, the public gradually became reassured and complaints about mistreatment tailed off. But not before we had weathered a storm involving the arrest and alleged beating up of a young man of mixed race who ended up in hospital. The policemen involved in the arrest said that the young man had injured himself while trying to get away. Friends and supporters of the young man declared he was punched and kicked in a police van. Two lay visitors went to see him in hospital. Of course, they could have no opinion about what had occurred but they appraised themselves of his condition and were satisfied that he was being well looked after though under guard in the hospital. The incident and the lay visitors involvement led to several stormy sessions for the Consultative Group. The Panel, however, had done its job - it had reacted to the welfare of the young man, it had given a factual report which had been made known through the Group. If the matter was to be pursued further it would come within the competence of the official complaints procedure.

The second beneficial effect of the Panel was the changes it inspired in the way prisoners were treated. Although specific ill-treatment of suspects was rare, there were a lot of oversights and anomalies in the custody arrangements. The Panel took up such questions as proper meals and exercise for suspects. Had a doctor been called when asked for? Were interpreters found quickly enough for those with little English? By stages, micro-wave ovens were installed, toilet and washing facilities were improved and a book service was set up by visitors to provide reading matter for suspects. The lay visitors scheme was inaugurated in the five Lambeth police stations in January, 1984. Like the Consultative Group itself, the Panel became the model for similar schemes throughout Britain. After seven years it is still able to recruit people to what is a time consuming and unglamorous task.

During the course of our early discussions on crime levels in the Borough, one of our responses was to form a "Serious Crimes Committee" to study the community's role in the fight against crime. It is worth emphasising at this point that although the Group had got much closer to the Police through regular contact with the officers who came to our meetings and although we had developed a sense of common cause in the need to combat the high levels of crime, including violent crime, we were also aware that we had to keep our distance. If we lost our sympathy with the feelings of people in the streets we would become useless. There were plenty of critics around who were very ready to accuse us of being a front for the Police. It is greatly to the credit of the Group throughout the various phases of its existence and in spite of all the pressures it was subject to that it never lost its reputation for being impartial and independent. At least, it never lost that reputation with the people of the Borough.

Crime prevention and political tangles

The Serious Crimes Committee was set up as the one permanent sub-committee of the Group and it was meant to be chaired ex officio by the Group's deputy chairman. This was not how things turned out and I was effectively its chairman for most of the first ten years. We had regular meetings with the Lambeth CID and were given dismaying statistics. We were all well aware that the greatest public anxiety was attached to robbery, burglary and car crime, for the most part in that order though for periods burglary changed places with robbery. The CID were generally successful in solving murders and rapes because information was more readily forthcoming but as time went on drug racketeering with its attendant violence became very difficult to deal with.

The committee did a lot of solid work agitating about improved lighting on housing estates and strengthening front doors and window catches. We made the first moves towards setting up neighbourhood watch schemes which gradually became a very broad movement and not only in middle class areas. We also made representations about the difficulties of obtaining insurance cover in Brixton. When the incidence of robbery on the Northern Line of the Underground mounted, we urged better co-operation between the Transport and the Metropolitan Police and we organised public meetings to articulate Tube travellers disquiet.

Another campaign, first raised in the Committee but soon to become a major concern of the Group as a whole, was the use of knives in street crime. There had been a steady escalation in the use of knives in robberies and there had been a number of particularly vicious stabbings, in some cases the victim had been cut after the money had been handed over. The chief superintendent in charge of one of our police stations was particularly exercised about the problem and, assisted by members of the Group, a poster campaign was launched graphically illustrating the consequences of knife attacks and carrying the message that those who carried knives were likely to use them when under pressure. At the same time there was a general call to dump knives and other sharp instruments in special containers in the streets. This campaign was a modest success: quite a lot of miscellaneous hardware was found in the boxes and for a while the use of knives in street robberies diminished. Perhaps more fundamentally, we joined with others in persuading the Home Secretary - now Douglas Hurd - to ban flick knives and to modify the law to presume that any one carrying a knife or sharp instrument over a certain size was committing an offence.

The Serious Crimes Committee accomplished two other notable projects though by the time in question, it had changed its name to "The Crime Prevention Committee". We conceived the idea of investigating a particular neighbourhood with a view to getting as accurate a picture as possible about the law and order situation there and about its quality of life. We chose a housing estate in the northern part of the Borough - it was a manageable size and the chairman of the tenants association who was a member of the Group was keen to co-operate. As soon as we announced our purpose and the locality, however, we ran into opposition from a local Borough councillor supported by the MP. It was never absolutely clear why they were so opposed. The probable reason was that the Council was unpopular on the estate and our investigation would have brought forth some severe criticisms.

The confrontation between the Consultative Group (which had endorsed the Committee's project) and the politicians was an instance of the deteriorating relationship of the Group with the governing Labour group of Lambeth Council. This particular dispute led to a very fraught session of the Consultative Group. Some of our members, urged on by the chairman of the tenants association of the aforesaid estate, were all for defying the politicians and carrying on with the investigation. I took the view that it was no part of the Group's purpose to go against the politicians in an issue that was less than a hanging matter. They were after all elected representatives of the people - we were not - and there were other housing estates. The issue went to one of our first votes

- nearly everything heretofore had been settled unanimously - and my position prevailed by one vote.

Lambeth Council did not stand high in the esteem of our members. At the beginning, Labour and Conservative councillors took a full part in all our proceedings. Lambeth's MPs (three Labour, one Conservative, to begin with - later reduced to three when one of the Labour held constituencies was abolished) were generous in their appearances. The Labour councillors eventually withdrew on an issue of Labour Party policy. Unlike all the provincial police forces, the Metropolitan Police was not under local control but was regulated directly by the Home Office. It was Labour's conviction that London's Police should come under the control of the then existing Greater London Council and that this local control should be paralleled in all the London boroughs. Accordingly, Lambeth set up a Police Committee to rival the Consultative Group. We were made to leave our office in the Town Hall and later we were denied the use of the Town Hall for our meetings. This was a very unhappy state of affairs. The Group needed to be in partnership with the Council and it was very proper that our meetings should be in the Town Hall - the civic centre of our borough. Given these political problems, it is even more remarkable that the Group achieved the success it has. It is fair to add, however, that by the time of the Group's tenth anniversary in March, 1992, there was some hope of the breach being healed.

Life on a Brixton housing estate

To return to the question of the housing estate enquiry. Not all the Labour councillors were completely negative with us. In an effort to conciliate some of them, we agreed to change the name of the Serious Crimes Committee to the Crime Prevention Committee - this was at their request. Under its new name the Committee obtained the co-operation of one of the Central Brixton Labour Councillors - one who had never ceased to support the Group despite the official line of his party and who eventually became the Group's chairman - for the investigation to be made on the Moorlands Estate in his ward.

We had to gain the agreement of the tenants. The chairman of the tenants association - a somewhat frail body - was enthusiastic. Under the aegis of the association, we held several public meetings to commend the idea of a comprehensive survey of the estate. We had signed up a professor of sociology in the University of London to prepare our questionnaire and to analyse the answers. We recruited a group of seminary students who were in London for a special part of their training to carry out the survey. Sixty per cent of the households on the estate were actually visited twice and the questionnaire completed in face to face conversation. Few surveys could have been as comprehensive as this one.

The survey and its analysis revealed a dismaying reality. Over half the households were single parent families living on income support. Nearly all those in work - a minority - wanted to move away at the first opportunity. Several of the dwellings were occupied by groups of squatters and one at least of these gave its neighbours an excruciating time. Robberies, molestations and burglaries were an almost daily occurrence. One lady confined to a wheel chair had watched local boys help themselves to her things no less than six times. A number of the tenants were people with special needs, most of them for psychiatric reasons. These were meant to have special care from social workers but it was never adequate. I visited an elderly Jamaican in one of the flats. He was an alcoholic and had nothing in his place but an old mattress and a few cooking pots. He was eventually found dead there.

The Moorlands was quite a new estate and there was a good variety of dwellings - houses with small gardens and small blocks of flats, none of them over three stories high - and it was attractively laid out. Indeed, at the time it was completed it won a prize for good municipal housing. Some of the architectural features, however, made for difficult maintenance and no one at that time planned housing schemes with crime prevention in mind. The Moorlands provided very convenient cover for house-breakers and lots of escape routes for muggers. Few residents used the garages provided for their cars - that would be an invitation for the vandals to wreck them.

Apart from the crime, the most insistent complaint of the residents was about delays in house repairs and the quality of the work when they were done. Our survey encouraged the Council with existing plans to set up a new estate office in an adjacent street and to separate repairs from general housing administration. I became convinced that housing should be taken out of the control of local authorities completely. The Police had three permanent beat officers covering the estate. These were doing a good job and we recommended that they should have an office on the estate which would be manned at certain known hours.

Our report which contained the analysis of the survey had a lot to say about the quality of life on the estate. Quite a lot of the individual homes were very nicely furnished and attractive to live in, but the communal areas were an absolute fright. Dirt and graffiti were everywhere and most lamps and trees had been vandalised. In terms of racial make-up, about forty per cent of the people were white, the majority, of other ethnic origins, were mainly West Indian but there were a good number of Asians too. Except for occasional upsets, they seemed to be no racial antagonisms. The over-riding problem of the estate was demoralisation.

Our report was well received by the people of the estate, by the Police and the Home Office and in academic departments. Our leading conclusion was that the people of the Moorlands should be enabled and encouraged to take possession of their estate. A certain amount of money could be well spent on improving communal facilities but more particularly a patient effort was required to help the residents to come out of their shells and discover themselves as a community. It was abundantly clear that nothing of any value would happen unless the people committed themselves to it.

One of the authors of our report was a young probation officer with a number of clients on the estate. He led an excellent effort to get together all "the professionals" who had an interest in the estate. These included the permanent beat policemen and women, teachers, clergy, school attendance officers, social workers including psychiatric specialists, housing officers - altogether, twelve or fifteen "professionals" came to the first consultative meetings. But true to the conclusion of our survey, they resolved that there had to be a joint effort with a representative group of the residents and nothing would be promoted without their understanding and co-operation. Indeed, the ideal was that the professionals would be at the service of the residents as they began to take charge of their own destiny.

The endeavour was a good one but unfortunately we were not able to sustain it. The clergy were moved and some of the most committed of the professionals were posted to other jobs. I myself became responsible for a community centre - St Vincents - only about 200 yards away from the estate but with a railway track separating them. There will be more about St Vincents later in this story. For the moment, I just have to record that this is where my energies were directed.

The anatomy of street crime

The other particular project that the Crime Prevention Committee accomplished was a study of street crime in Lambeth. This enquiry occupied us for most of 1988/9. We enlisted the expertise of Mrs Elizabeth Burney, a sociologist specialising in criminal matters at Goldsmiths College, in South East London, who was already associated with us as a lay visitor to police stations. Elizabeth Burney was given access to police records, she spoke to probation officers and some young offenders in their care. She also studied various schemes for the rehabilitation of youngsters convicted of street crime, especially the Battersea Basement Project which had a very imaginative education and training programme. Her report was presented to the Consultative Group in full session in March of 1990.

It was not a surprise that most street robberies in Lambeth were committed by black teenagers and that central Brixton and parts of Clapham were the high risk places. But it was a surprise that old people were a small proportion of the victims - press horror stories of elderly people constantly attacked after collecting their pensions had created a very distorted picture. Women returning home from work were most vulnerable to handbag snatches. Most attacks with violence occurred late at night and were perpetrated mainly against young people - boys and girls - returning home from social events.

A lot of muggings were committed by comparatively few miscreants. Most of them gave up the activity by the time they were twenty-one. Why did they get into mugging people? Elizabeth Burney's study found no great correlation with broken homes or drug taking. There was a very clear link with under-achieving at school, macho tendencies and truancy. The boys mugged people basically for the money, though the excessive violence aspect was generally a form of self display too, and the money was most often spent on expensive clothes, including trainers at over £100 a pair.

The courts nearly always gave custodial sentences for young street robbers. Elizabeth Burney questioned whether this was appropriate treatment. The Battersea Basement Project had indicated to her that a good number of the offending youngsters could be weaned away from crime if they were helped to find prospects in other directions. The importance of good black role models was also stressed in the report. And another of her wise and compassionate findings was the importance of support for families whose youngsters were going astray.

At roughly the same time that Elizabeth Burney's Street Crime Report was presented, the Brixton division of the Police, with the highest mugging rate in the country, came up with the BAR project ("Brixton Against Robbery"). The great virtue of this initiative was the recruitment of an ex-mugger to get among the boys and a very street-wise young woman to make contact with the families. This indeed was one of the most encouraging of late nineteen-eighties developments - the emergence of young black adults, some of them professionally trained, who were prepared to take responsibility for delinquent black youngsters.

Racism in the police

Early in the life of the Consultative Group, one of our members showed a particular concern about racist attitudes on the part of the average police officer. It was clear that official Force policy was entirely non-discriminatory and yet reports of insulting and provocative behaviour by police officers on the streets were so persistent. Maybe something was amiss with police training. As a result of this suspicion being raised in the Group, arrangements were made for members of the Group to sit in on the relevant sessions of the Hendon Police College's courses. These sessions were originally called "human awareness" training, later they were dubbed "policing skills". The main criticism that our people made of the training was that there was scarcely any participation in it of black people. As a consequence, young police recruits were given only a very theoretical and superficial understanding of ethnic values. And seeing that a large number of recruits to the Metropolitan Police came from outside the London area and indeed from outside any big city, they were often quite unprepared for the social make-up of the metropolis and quite startled by the tensions they encountered on the streets. In this situation what was called the "canteen culture" of the police force became decisive. Whatever good will young policemen and women had when they started was quickly dissipated by the hostility they frequently encountered. Acquiring no depth of understanding and meeting black people only in confrontations, they simply adopted an attitude of "them and us".

These criticisms were accompanied by proposals that much more inter-racial encounter should be built into the courses and that there should be a lot more in-service training in racial awareness. The report which our Hendon visitors prepared was duly presented at one of the Group's regular meetings in the presence of the commandant of the College. The Wimbledon tennis was on at the time and from the chair I remarked that his response was a "hard return of service". His reaction was a pity for the report was sympathetic to efforts that were already being made and both the criticisms and the proposals were closely argued and modest in their scope. Nine years later another visit was paid to Hendon and substantially the same criticisms were made with very similar proposals. This time, they were accepted in their entirety by a senior officer from Scotland Yard.

Allied to this issue of racial awareness training has been the question of ethnic recruitment into the Police. During the eighties both Scotland Yard and senior officers of the Lambeth Police stepped up their efforts to attract black and Asian recruits. They have had very modest success and worse than the reluctance to join has been the high proportion of resignations among the few that did join. In the mid-eighties, in a Force of 28,000 officers less than 500 were black or Asian. To reflect the ethnic make-up of London's population, 5,000 would have been a more adequate proportion. Some of us in the Consultative Group tried to get behind this cause. We organised several meetings between black young people and young police officers and we had two major semi-recruitment meetings set up jointly by our Catholic chaplaincy and a thriving Pentecostal church in Brixton. The central recruitment department of the Police sent down a team which included a very on-the-spot and personable black

102

woman officer but it was clear that some of her white colleagues were a long way from understanding what the problems were. These meetings, attended by black adults as well as black youngsters, endorsed the idea that ethnic recruitment would be a very good thing but we cannot say that they produced any new recruits. Probably, a reasonable level of ethnic recruitment will have to wait until more black and Asian young people find a better sense of belonging in Britain. Certainly there could be a number of excellent candidates from our Caribbean community. The present number of persevering black police officers is small, but there is no doubt about their quality.

An extension of local democracy

On March 3rd, 1992, the Consultative Group reached its tenth birthday. To have survived so long is in itself a considerable testimony of its value. Given the tensions in Brixton following the 1981 riots and the complete breakdown of community/police relations, few people would have given the Group a life expectancy of ten weeks. Against all the odds, there is no doubt that it has done a great deal to improve community relations in Lambeth. The police divisions have quietly made themselves accountable to it. Everyone in the Borough knows where to come if there is trouble or complaint. Still after ten years the monthly meetings are well attended and there is a steady increase in the number of Lambeth organisations that affiliate to it. In the late summer of 1985, the second Brixton upheaval and the Broadwater Farm explosion in North London occurred at roughly the same time. Broadwater Farm has remained in a state of partial emergency virtually ever since. In Brixton, dismaying as the recurrence was, life returned to normal within a few days. The Group was a very important means by which the community was able to live through its anger, distress and fear.

It can also be said that the Group discovered a new dimension to local democracy. The community must have the Police Force for its very security and well being. But if the consent and the co-operation of the people is withdrawn the Police can scarcely do its job. This was acutely the case in Brixton before the Group came onto the scene. The frank and persevering dialogue that began on March 3rd, 1982, gradually transformed the situation. After a year or more it was possible to detect that the police representatives had lost their original scepticism and were looking to us for signs of public approval. Moreover the proceedings at our meetings were an exercise in democratic exchange. Any properly constituted Lambeth organisation which accepted our terms of reference could affiliate, any member of the public could come and speak. And certainly at the beginning, the great majority of our decisions were taken unanimously. As a result, good feeling prevailed even in the midst of fierce argument. We had to recognise that, as in industrial relations, there were two sides to the table but this did not obscure the fact that we shared a common purpose.

It may be that the discovery of the Lambeth Consultative Group could be formulated into a principle: that wherever the community needs a professional service, it is an excellent thing if the providers of the service can be accountable to its consumers and if the consumers can learn to appreciate what it costs to provide the service and play a part in improving it. In the abnormal conditions of Lambeth in the eighties, the Consultative Group led the way in dialogue with the Police. Other mechanisms could be found for popular participation in the Health Service, Education, the Social Services and even the Legal system.

Though the Consultative Group is a success story, the economic and social consequences of the disturbances have been grievous. Brixton became synonymous with trouble and decay. A lot of families moved away and many of those who remained only did so out of necessity as we saw when we were discussing the Moorlands estate. Business too ebbed away. Soon after the first lot of riots the chain businesses with branches in Brixton got together to launch the "We're backing Brixton" campaign. This was a valuable holding operation and still to this day some firms have held out in Brixton really, one suspects, against their better economic judgement. The markets in central Brixton used to be among the best and cheapest shopping centres in South London. They are still good and cater well for the nearby community but fewer people come into Brixton to shop than once was the case. A number of what were once smart shops are now occupied by cut price dealers. But this is not quite the whole story. There are signs of the emergence of a better Brixton.

Rehabilitation of the "Front Line"

The central Brixton area with Railton Road as its spine went through various changes of mood in the aftermath of the 1981 riots. There was a heady sense of victory over the Police to begin with. The illegal shebeens flourished, drug dealing went on virtually unimpeded and the whole area became unmanageable for the ordinary processes of law and order. Mention has been made of the Consultative Group's efforts to set up an interchange between some of the "Front-liners" and the Police with a view to relocating the shebeens and bringing them into some sort of legality. The Council's demolitions of the shebeens on November 1st, 1982, and the successful handling of the disturbance that ensued that evening, was seen by the Police as a regaining of the initiative. Moreover, the Police became more sure that a substantial number of local residents were veering to their side because a group of them had complained about the lawlessness at meetings of the Consultative Group. With a renewed sense of confidence, the Police began to squeeze the drug traffickers and the market began to disperse. At the same time, the co-operation of local people was encouraged by a series of very good permanent beat police officers.

Environmental improvements

These delicate signs of better things were rudely dissipated by the further big eruption of September, 1985. Once again, Brixton was in a state of emergency. Surprisingly, however, there was no return to the near anarchy that had followed the 1981 upheaval. A lot of delicate repair work had to be done again but it was clear enough that the area had developed a taste for peace and good order and the hard men were becoming more isolated. Life was back to normal within very few days. The Council had already initiated some notable environmental improvements. The sites of the demolished shebeens and a little slip road beside them had been transformed into the "Dexter Road Piazza". True, the naughty boys kept up the trade in drugs in the new and more gracious setting of the piazza and there was an attempt to set up an unsightly lean-to in one corner for some kind of trading initiative. But with seats and lamp standards and some vulnerable trees, official recognition had been paid to the social value of the Front-Line area.

Things seldom come right all at once. Certain of the habitués took to setting up powerful sound systems in the piazza at weekends and these blighted the lives of the local residents for a while. This was another complaint raised at a Consultative Group meeting and a combination of an exercise of the Council's noise regulations, patient policing and local indignation shortly got rid of the nuisance. The sound systems were replaced by regular weekend evangelistic services by black Pentecostal congregations which were more acceptable to the people.

Another Council improvement was the completion of the very attractive Marcus Garvey housing estate just opposite the piazza on Railton Road. Marcus Garvey was a significant figure in the growth of black consciousness. He was a Jamaican who spent a lot of his life in the United States but eventually settled in Britain. This was in the early part of this century. It was Marcus Garvey who first proclaimed to the black people of the Americas that they should look for their identity in Africa. In this he was part of the inspiration of the cult of Rastafari and in Alex Haley's *Roots*, his message of African identity has been given memorable expression.

The naming of the estate was an instance of Lambeth Council's very positive attitude to race relations and did them great credit. Not so good was the history of the "Afro-Caribbean Cultural Centre" a little further up Railton Road. After the first lot of riots, there was a lot of discussion about the building of a grand cultural centre for black people in Brixton. It was rumoured that the government was prepared to put up a lot of money for the purpose. The government's commitment proved to be a lot less certain than that of Lambeth Council. Even so, the best that the Council could do was to erect and equip a large prefabricated wooden structure on ground in Railton Road which had recently been cleared near the Marcus Garvey site. This building, styled the "Afro-Caribbean Cultural Centre" became known as "the hut". It was opened with a municipal fanfare, a considerable number of local dignitaries joined a large assembly of Front-liners and the bar was manned by police officers from the community involvement team. It was an auspicious beginning to a well meaning project.

By 1986, however, "the hut" had degenerated into another drug market. Dealers congregated in the street outside, ordinary people made diversions if they could to avoid the place. The Police decided that a big raid was called for. This was one of their operations that they could not broadcast in advance but prior notice was given to the current chairperson and the secretariat of the Consultative Group. The raid was labelled "Operation Condor". Over a thousand officers were mobilised, most of them in reserve but several hundreds were immediately engaged. "The hut" backs onto a railway line. A special train was employed to pull up behind on an embankment and to disgorge officers. At the critical moment, two pantechnicons drew up at the roadside and out leapt another squad of officers. They all fell on the hut and in no time had arrested about eighty people including a mother and two children. Drug packets were all over the place, a hand gun was found, and at the back by the embankment innumerable handbags and discarded contents.

There was a long line of police officers forming a ring about a hundred yards from the action. One of these was a black officer. He got a barrage of insults from the crowd that gathered but was commended afterwards for his steadfastness. The planning officers had also taken care to inform the public what was going on. Leaflets were distributed to all by-standers to tell them that this was an operation to attack the drug menace and make Brixton safer for law abiding citizens. There was no doubt that most local residents applauded the operation. Even some of the Front-liners surrounding a permanent beat officer whom they knew well and protesting about this invasion of their territory were able to listen to his arguments that this was a case when the Police were doing what was undoubtedly their proper job.

The careful planning and the number of officers engaged illustrates the precarious state of law and order in Brixton in the mid-eighties. One prominent black lady who lived just off Railton Road described the scene graphically to me afterwards. With the train, the pantechnicon, the cohorts of police officers, she said "it was like the wild west!" But although the Police took a sledge hammer to crack a nut on this occasion, no one could say their precautions were unwise. The operation succeeded in moving the drug scene on to fresh fields. No big drug baron was among those arrested. The Police showed determination in the face of a drug menace that was growing and becoming ever more vicious but still their intelligence left a lot to be desired. Alas, "the hut" never reopened. It gradually mouldered away and eventually it was demolished.

The "Front-line" began to lose its menace and one heard the name less and less. The focus of the drug scene shifted a few streets away to what was called the "barrier block" but the associated crime became much more diffused. Every now and again in the Consultative Group we used to celebrate a downturn in the street robbery figures but these improvements were generally short lived. The Police gradually learned how to contain the problem and the sociology of youthful black crime became better understood. Mrs Elizabeth Burney's survey and the launch of the BAR project already discussed were stages in this. Brixton had been top of the national league in street crime for a very long time but in March, 1990, it was overtaken by Hackney.

Although the crime figures improved, the economic consequences of the riots persisted. But some gains were made. Tesco opened a big new supermarket near the centre of Brixton. No doubt the Council provided some inducements for this. It meant several hundred new jobs but it is not certain how many of these went to local people and it is doubtful if other businesses in Brixton benefitted by it. Most of the customers seem to go in and out by car. Nevertheless, its opening was a big sign of new life. Allied Carpets came too, and the Council opened an enterprise centre for a cluster of small businesses in the refurbished premises of the old Bon Marché department store in the main shopping centre. The "George" in Railton Road was one of the casualties of the 1981 riots - it was completely burnt down. In December, 1986. it reopened as "Mingles", a smart new pub and brasserie managed by one of Brixton's rugged personalities, Lloyd Leon. There is a "Mingles" in Kingston, Jamaica, where Lloyd Leon hails from. This was a reason for choosing the name but more particularly it declared a social purpose. "Mingles" was to bring all sections of the community together.

I always think of Lloyd Leon as the Gerry Fitt of the Front-line area. As Gerry Fitt was honest and brave enough sometimes to stand out against the corporate sentiments of the Belfast Catholic community that he represented, so Lloyd Leon on occasions spoke vehemently against black lawlessness. As a consequence, he was attacked one day in the pub by a group of young fellows and could have been badly hurt. Having been a Labour councillor for a number of years, he became the Mayor of Lambeth and in 1990 he succeeded to the chairmanship of the Consultative Group.

St Vincent's Community Centre

Another fruitful development was the reorientation of St Vincent's centre in Talma Road, one block over from Railton Road and adjacent to the new piazza. This was an old back street mission of the last century built by the central Brixton Anglican church, St Matthews. It had become redundant in the nineteen-sixties and was acquired by a Catholic charitable organisation called the Society of St Vincent de Paul (the SVP). The Society set it up as a centre for deaf and dumb people in London and gave it a new name, St Vincent's.

By the mid nineteen-eighties, the deaf community were using the building minimally. It was located in the Brixton heartland and the streets were not safe for incoming people. Yet the centre was ideally located to be a community focus for the old Front-line area. At first I negotiated with the existing management committee for occasional use of the building. This did not work out very well because there were always problems about opening and shutting it after occasional lettings. It was later intimated that the deaf wanted to move elsewhere and the SVP would probably dispose of the building. At this point, I suggested to the central board of the Society that I and a local committee would be ready to take over the management of St Vincent's as a general community centre for the neighbourhood. We would keep the deaf community in their present use of the building but if the arrangement gave our local committee responsibility for all the running costs then we would have to charge the deaf a rent. The times of occupation were all agreed and likewise a low figure for the rent. But, alas, the deaf were used to having exclusive use of the building and having the major bills settled by the SVP. In spite of our agreement, they were not satisfied with the arrangement and after six months they did move out.

It was a shame that we were not able to reach a modus vivendi with the deaf but their departure did give the new committee unrestricted use of the building. We started off

111

with a mothers' and toddlers' club and a Sunday afternoon evangelistic service. The former was run by a young local mother assisted by other young mums and it had quite a good run. The service was a noble try but never got beyond the small group of black and white people who actually promoted it. After about nine months it transferred as a prayer group to the home of some religious sisters who lived in the neighbourhood. Later, we let it on Sunday afternoons to a local Pentecostal congregation who packed the place!

In the beginning we had a small committee of mainly local residents, a paid cleaner and £10,000 in the bank given to us by a small charitable trust. The core of our committee consisted of myself as chairman, a nun belonging to another religious community as secretary, a young accountant as treasurer and the young mother who ran the mothers' and toddlers' club. We had always wanted the committee to reflect the make-up of the local community and by stages we achieved this. We had also declared that we were a Christian service to the neighbourhood; we had a strong Catholic participation in the management but our committee members and our users covered a wide Christian spectrum and some had no declared religious allegiance.

Shortly after we took the building over, the Catholic Association for Racial Justice (CARJ) rented our one large committee room as its national office. We were very happy to have CARJ in residence because its purpose and our's were very much in line with one another. For a while, we also rented a small room as the regional office of the Catholic Fund for Overseas Development (CAFOD).

Little by little, we extended the scope of the centre. An early imperative had been a renovation and redecoration of the whole building. This was undertaken by Cathedral Employment Enterprises (CEE), which began as a community employment project but which later ramified into a major voluntary training agency. Included in CEE's services was a network of "job clubs" and one of these found a home at St

Vincent's for over three years. Our job club was open four mornings a week for all comers. It had an excellent manager, an Irishman, who took endless pains over his very varied clientele, some of whom had not had a job for years. A very large number of long-term unemployed, men and women, did get jobs or training through his efforts. One of his clients was an Iranian refugee who seemed to regard the club as his family and its manager as his uncle. Sadly he was one who still had not been placed when the club was taken away from St Vincent's. The Department of Employment officials decided that job clubs should be in high street, not in church hall-type, premises. Ours moved to Streatham - CEE continued to run it, though with different staff, but we were very sad that it was lost to us and to Brixton.

By this time we had been able to appoint a full-time caretaker and a part-time "community centre development officer". We were very fortunate to receive a number of generous grants from charitable trusts. Some of these enabled us to take on our staff; others helped us to make further capital improvements and to acquire more furniture and equipment. After about three years we were able to keep pace with ordinary running costs with rental income from our users but we have never been able to pay for salaries and improvements without charitable money. In addition to these gifts, we were also given large sums by five charities for the replacement of the roof. Our committee knew this was needed when we took over the building. This money together with a large grant from Lambeth's Inner City Partnership programme enabled us to embark on this work early in 1992.

Our caretaker, born in Jamaica, lives just opposite the centre. Though his constant attendance and obvious devotion to St Vincent's can sometimes be mistaken for a sense of ownership, the centre could scarcely be better looked after. Our first Development Officer was a professional social worker, a lady born in Trinidad, who was able to give us just two days a week which, happily, was the amount of her time that we could pay for. She was with us for eighteen months and initiated several excellent projects some of which came to fulfilment after she had left us. Her successor was a married man with two young children, like our caretaker born in Jamaica, who, as a mature student engaged in a business studies course, was glad of a two-day a week appointment. He too has done a great deal to enhance the use of the centre.

St Vincent's has got steadily busier. A boys and girls karate class meets twice a week. We have a steel band group that rises and falls. A local resident is a theatrical agent and we accommodate rehearsals for her companies, one of which performs English language plays in Germany. We have had a Tai Chi group and Aerobics and many occasional lettings, including anti-poll tax meetings, gatherings of the local residents association and numerous private parties. Weekends are a continuous performance. Two Pentecostal congregations meet on Sundays; we have two friendly societies, one with a fortnightly and the other with a monthly meeting on Saturdays, and there is a Saturday and a Sunday meeting of "Narcotics Anonymous" (NA). The Sunday evening NA meeting is attended by seldom less than 50 young people, mainly white but some black. They allow me to join the meeting once a month and I marvel at the work of redemption that they are bringing to each other. Every meeting brings forth heart breaking personal stories. Each of them has suffered grievously from self-loathing and near despair. For them all NA is a lifeline. They stand in constant peril of relapse. At the meetings, they submit to a discipline that most of them would never have entertained in the days of their "using". They also show marvellous affection for one another. I have often thought that accommodating NA would alone justify the existence of St Vincent's. In fact the St Vincent's meeting is one of about six others taking place every Sunday evening and there is a similar number of meetings available on any evening of the week. Our Sunday evening meeting, however, is one of the biggest.

At the beginning of 1992, St Vincent's was preparing to launch a "sanctuary scheme" for mentally disturbed people of which there are many in Brixton. For some years, our committee had wanted to make a contribution to "care in the community" for the large numbers of men and women who were being released from mental hospitals. We had organised a short run of afternoon craft classes as a pilot scheme and these were sufficiently successful for us to want to go further. The demise of our job club giving us spare capacity and an encounter with an organisation called "Lambeth Link" which was already working with mentally disturbed people, gave us our opportunity. We were awarded a substantial government grant via Lambeth Social Services to provide a day centre with a full-time worker for five days a week. The ground floor of our building including the kitchen would be devoted to the scheme. At the time of writing the project was about to be born. It promises to make the lives of a lot of very vulnerable people a little more secure.

Several of our benefactors had asked us for an appraisal of the work of St Vincent's. With the assurance of some further charitable money for the purpose, we had this professionally carried out at the end of 1991. Our appraiser had some valuable suggestions about improving our management structure but he was keenest on our developing our links with the local community still further. We had been inhibited by the precariousness of our finances which meant among other constraints that we could afford only a two-day a week development officer. We could now justify a full-time appointment if we had the money. It was clear enough from the appraisal that St Vincent's was well placed to make an even greater contribution to community development in our neighbourhood. The old Front-line area with all its distresses and waywardness could steadily be rehabilitated for the benefit of all its people.

Councillor Sam King, Jamaican born and ex-RAF, who became the first black Mayor of the London Brough of Southwark.

Multi-racial progress

Brixton and the Front-line in some way symbolise the state of race relations in Britain. The situation is ambiguous - in some ways better in some ways worse. The riots signalled to the nation that younger generations of black people were not going to accept anything less than complete parity of esteem and equality of opportunity in Britain. By the early nineteen-nineties we have made a little progress. Four "ethnic" MPs were elected in the 1987 general election, all dependent on a large number of white votes, and this increased to six in the 1992 election. The largest trade union in the country, the Transport and General Workers, elected a black general secretary; in the same year, a black woman barrister became a QC. These could scarcely be labelled "token" appointments. In each case the recipients of these distinctions had conspicuous personal qualities. In an early post-war election, a black candidate for a South London constituency lost a safe seat purely on a racist vote. He had had a distinguished political career in the West Indies and subsequently rose to great eminence in this country. But at the time of this particular election, he was not acceptable to the South London voters simply because he was black. This is much less likely to happen now. Indeed, a prominent member of a constituency party in the white redoubt of Cheltenham recently made a fool of himself by opposing the nomination of a black candidate on thinly veiled racial grounds.

Britain is gradually getting used to prominent black people and is learning to take pride in them. Successful black sportsmen and women in the livery of Great Britain and big names in entertainment and music are now regarded as part of "us". It was very remarkable that the England test cricket team of 1991 playing against the West Indies included three black players and an Asian one. West Indian cricket fans were bemused to see their all-conquering heroes beginning to succumb to black players in the England side. However, black people for their part are not happy if their reputation in society depends predominantly on sport and entertainment. There is in fact a much broader base to black achievement. More and more black young people are entering management and the professions via higher education. They are still too few but significant numbers are blazing the trail.

The rise of black graduates

This highly desirable development is typified by the Vice-chairman of the St Vincent's Community Centre management committee. Aged around thirty, he is Brixton born of Jamaican parents. He was educated at a local comprehensive school, won a place at Oxford University and came away with a good degree and lots of success in university politics. Since then, he has worked in public relations for several London boroughs and is co-author of a book about black women serving in the British forces during the Second World War. Though not a Catholic, he has taken part in various studies under the auspices of the Catholic Bishops' Conference, including an equal opportunities declaration which the bishops were happy to endorse. He also belongs to our Congress Group.

One of his tasks while working for Lambeth Council was to organise the fortieth anniversary celebrations of the arrival of the troopship "Empire Windrush", the Mayflower of black immigration into Britain. She docked at Tilbury on June 22nd, 1948, with 500 Jamaican settlers on board. A number of these pioneers found a home in Brixton and it is another plus point for Lambeth Council that it made a lot of this anniversary.

At first, many black graduates inclined towards public sector employment - partly for idealistic reasons and partly because they were more sure of a welcome there than in business. This gradually changed in the eighties and I began to meet more and more gifted and well-educated young black

118

people who were successfully competing in industry and commerce. It has to be said, though, they often had to endure high levels of stress. We still have to see how far they will be able to rise. Business with strict cost effectiveness criteria ought to be fairly immune from artificial prejudice, but top jobs may prove very tough citadels to breach. All the same, the levels of success already attained do testify to the fact that management in commerce and industry as well as in government service is open to qualified and hard working young people of all races.

It remains true, however, that the education system has failed for many black youngsters. We have seen how under-achievement at school is a very significant conditioning factor towards teenage delinquency. As a nation we accord a value to the most talented of our young people and spend a lot of money on higher education for them. Some black youngsters are benefitting from this. but the majority do not get the impression that society values them and wants to develop their talents. Black youngsters are particularly prone to self doubt. Without encouragement and without rigorous expectations of them by their teachers, many find it easy to "cop-out". And it has to be said that many white teachers have found black youngsters difficult to manage. In general, it seems to be true that the very progress we make creates further expectations. Building a multi-racial society is a very complex task and maybe we should not be too discontented with the modest results we have accomplished so far.

Visit to North America

I had been thinking for some time that in the quest for a multi-racial society in Britain we had a lot to learn from North America where black people had been indigenous in a white society for a lot longer than here. I was delighted when I got the chance to visit Canada and the United States in October, 1984. I had just two weeks in Montreal and Ontario and another two weeks in the eastern part of the United

119

States. In Canada, I was able to take in the fact that here was a nation with two basic cultures - British and French. Having successfully made a nation out of two proud and contrasting European traditions, Canada had also learned how to accommodate other races and cultures. It helps, of course, that she has a lot of space and needs people. But while I was there I was able to catch a glimpse of how two of her ethnic minorities - her "native people" or Indians and her Mennonite community, including the "old order" Mennonites - were faring.

The Indians of the Iroquois group of tribes were hanging on to a segregated existence in the midst of modern Ontario. Maybe in the great spaces of western and northern Canada, other Indian tribes could live a more traditional life. What I saw of the Iroquois made me wonder what the best interest of their people was. Surely they had to retain their identity and values but had they any future separated from the dominant culture of Canada? The same question could be asked of the Mennonites. These are the descendants of the Anabaptists of sixteenth century Switzerland who came to Canada from Pennsylvania following the War of Independence. Whenever questions of adaptation to the North American way of life arise there is always a schism. Some Mennonites have conformed to Canadian culture almost completely and their Mennonite worship at church is not much different from a Methodist-type service. Other communities of Mennonites worship in the beautiful austere clapper-board chapels characteristic of the Sect but have compromised with the Canadian way of life to the extent of having cars, though with all the chrome parts blacked out. The strict "old order" Mennonites still retain seventeenth century costume and travel by horse and buggy. They deny themselves electricity, depending on oil lamps for their lighting and wood fuel for their cooking and heating. Nevertheless, they farm extremely well and as a community are virtually self sufficient. Canadian law requires them to send their children to school but the "old order" families withdraw their young people from the education system at the first opportunity. This and the general sealed nature of the community leads to the steady loss of their young people.

I was enormously impressed by the way Canada leaves a multitude of ethnic and cultural communities virtually undisturbed. There is a great respect on the part of the generality of Canadians for the rights of minorities. The Indian peoples have lots of friends and defenders and in the far frozen north nobody is allowed to push the "Inuit" (Eskimo) people around. I was particularly interested in how immigrants from the West Indies were doing. I spent an evening with a family I knew well in Trinidad. They lived in a pleasant small housing scheme within the orbit of Toronto. Their neighbours included families from Newfoundland (a relatively depressed part of Canada), the Philippines, Dominica, Jamaica, Vietnam and India. At the time of my visit there was plenty of work and good wages. My friends' children were all doing well at school and each one expected to go to college and have good opportunities for their careers. In general, Caribbean immigrants seemed to have a good reputation. There are some poor black people in Canada; Toronto has an area known as Jane-Finch which is the nearest Canada has to a black ghetto. There is a Caribbean Catholic Cultural Centre there run by a priest from Trinidad. Canada has a liberal immigration policy but she has been selective in a way that Britain never was. Her doors are open to people with skills. So the effect of her policy is to cream off a lot of capable people, such as my Trinidadian friends, from the Caribbean. Large numbers of Guyanese have found their way to Canada. They have been escaping from the gross mismanagement of the home economy as well as being attracted by opportunity in North America.

Canada is a mosaic of peoples and cultures; the United States is a melting pot. There the pressure to become just "American" is very much greater. It is true that a lot of people carry double identities - Italian-American,

121

Black-American and so on - but it is the American part that counts. In Buffalo in New York State, I attended a Mass organised by the National Office of Black Catholics - a group of downtown parishes had combined to promote it. The Mass included a slide show giving the history of black belonging in the Catholic Church - all the way from St Augustine in North Africa in the fourth century to St Martin of Porres in South America in the 17th and St Charles Lwanga in Uganda in the 19th. The Catholic community of the United States is working hard to dispel the notion that black people are protestants by nature. It is perfectly true that in the United States the protestant churches, and particularly the Baptists, were the main evangelising force for the black community people in the southern states. But in modern America there is a considerable movement of black people into the Catholic Church. The Mass I went to in Buffalo was clearly part of an evangelistic effort.

In general, the United States is way ahead of Britain in the development of a multi-racial society. Maybe this is only to be expected in a country which has had a large black presence for a lot longer than we have. At the same time there are no memories of slave relationships in Britain, though there are of colonial relationships. On the whole black people have benefitted from the liberalism of British society. However, toleration is one thing, positive acceptance - to say nothing of actual welcome - is quite another. The white people of the United States moved from negative and sometimes hostile attitudes to positive and generous attitudes under pressure from the civil rights movement led by the Reverend Martin Luther King, and from a wise response by President Lyndon Johnson's administration to the fierce race riots in American cities in the sixties.

At the same time, there were certain crucial Supreme Court decisions favouring multi-racial development. These departures have meant recognition for black (also for Hispanic) people at all official events, local and national, and a very broad advance by them into the professions, management and government. Many large American cities elect black mayors and the day cannot be too far away before there will be a black candidate for the presidency. In Britain, we have found it difficult to recruit black young people into the Police Force and recruitment into the Armed Forces has been very sparse. In the United States a number of major cities either have or have had black police chiefs and their Armed Forces have been a power house of black achievement. At the time of the Gulf War, the chief of their general staff was a black soldier, the son of Jamaican immigrants.

Integral development

In Britain, we need the talent of all our people and we have to evoke and nurture it. Market forces go some way towards encouraging and rewarding talent, but there is scope too for positive action on the part of government. If, as a nation, we valued our young people - all of them - adequately, we would do a lot more to see that they were properly educated and trained. The base line of progress is a determined policy of equal opportunity. But going along with this, we need positive discrimination in   certain key areas. Sometimes action is necessary to remove barriers. There is reason to believe that this is the case in the Armed Forces and the Police. There are other fields where imagination and generosity would make a lot of difference. This may be true in the legal profession and in the financial world. In some ways, racial prejudice - including the unconscious kind - is an aggravation of our long standing class consciousness. The latter is a stubborn and debilitating feature of British life but it is steadily being eroded in the late twentieth century. All facets of racial prejudice must go the same way and quicker if possible.

Maybe our progress in Britain compared with the United States and Canada is slow but integral. A sign of this is the performance of St Francis Xavier's Sixth Form College at Clapham in South London. It opened in 1985 as part of a far-reaching reorganisation of Catholic education in South West London. In the sixties, it could not be said that Catholic schools were in the van of multi-racial development. Now the situation is transformed and St Francis Xavier's is a manifest example of it. The College opened with 400 students; in September, 1991, there were 730 on the roll and this during the high period of shrinkage in the teenage population. The College is fed by eight Catholic secondary schools and it attracts a considerable number of young people from outside its catchment area, including a number of non-Catholics. The student body is a true reflection of the spectrum of young life in South West London as the 1980s gives way to the 1990s. And full virtue is made of its ethnic and cultural diversity. At the inaugural service in December, 1985, prayers were said in the languages of a wide range of parental belongings, including patois from the Eastern Caribbean. All races and cultures have contributed to the academic success of the College and the same is true in sport and extra-curricular activities.

As yet, there are too few ethnic or cultural minority teachers but the good-will exists for them and in time candidates of the right quality will apply. There are two governors of Caribbean origin and another from Mauritius. A significant sign of the harmony and purposefulness of St Francis Xavier's is that the buildings have suffered scarcely any damage or graffiti.

Conversions and vocations

Another sign of integral progress from a Catholic perspective is the steady number of black people who are becoming Catholics through the parishes. We have a programme called the RCIA - Rite of Christian Initiation for Adults. Through RCIA courses in parishes, adults interested in the Catholic faith are taken step by step to the point where they are ready to become members of the Church, either by reception if they are already baptised in another Christian church or by adult baptism if they have never belonged to any church before. Each year since its inception in 1987, between one and two hundred people throughout South London and Kent have joined the Church. This is a small beginning but a significant aspect of the influx is that between one third and one half have been black people. Our chaplaincy has made a modest contribution; parish life has been the path by which most of these new Catholics have found faith.

Young people seem particularly difficult to reach these days. Even youngsters from practising Catholic families, who have been to good Catholic schools and belong to lively and caring parishes are giving up the practice of their faith, at least temporarily. It is possible to be too depressed about this. A lot of youngsters who lapse find their way back in their twenties. All the Catholic influence they have received seldom goes for nothing, unless some special disaster occurs. The situation of young people on the margins of the Church, whose family influence is weak and who may have missed good Catholic schooling is, alas, very precarious spiritually. Nevertheless, it has always been true that every generation has to be converted afresh. I have a tremendous regard for the Young Christian Workers movement because I have found that it is capable of helping young people to make this second conversion.

A consequence of the relatively low levels of practice on the part of young people is that vocations to the priesthood and the religious life are sparse at that age. It is highly desirable that our black youngsters do discover vocations. It is easier for the moment for older people to fend off the allurements of the material order. They have inhabited it and maybe tasted its charms but they have realised that man does not live by bread alone. There is an important field of recruitment in the Catholic Church for mature married men in the permanent diaconate. As already mentioned, in Southwark Archdiocese we have five "ethnic" deacons of which two are from the Caribbean. In the matter of attracting young men

125

into the priesthood, I think our best expectation is of those who have pursued some other career before they offer themselves. These will have acquired an important degree of maturity and their gift of themselves can be more deliberate and thoroughgoing.

We did have one such man in South London, a very gifted person born in St Lucia but educated in Britain. However, he conceived his vocation in terms of St Lucia - he was trained and ordained in Rome and apart from temporary ministrations in South London while visiting his family he has always worked in St Lucia. It has been different with Howard James, born in London of Jamaican parents who was ordained to the priesthood for Westminster Archdiocese in December, 1991. Howard is our first "home grown" black priest. All of us are frail and capable of failure, but Howard looks to be a fine trail blazer as well as a most promising priest in his own right. Perhaps we should simply give thanks that such a young man has joined the priesthood and we can also be pleased that he is black. A very important part of our aspirations for a multi-racial society is that everyone will be accepted first for their personal qualities, their ethnic characteristics come later. The idea of integral progress in race relations is contained within the title of this story - "Some of us are Black". We are winning as we approach the conviction that we all belong together as sons and daughters of God. The Catholic community has a special opportunity to lead the nation in this realisation. The very name "Catholic" means universal and we have the highest Gospel warrant to be committed to a common belonging. Moreover, in this country a large proportion of "new Britons" have their roots in Catholic cultures.

But as a nation, we have not yet carried this message into the hearts of the generality of black young people, and, with different nuances, the same is true of young Asians. Most youngsters of Afro-Caribbean origin identify black; they are not yet sure of their British belonging. At one of our youth events, we organised a debate on the motion "Black and

British is a contradiction in terms". The small number taking part passed the motion by one vote despite arguments about the legal status of those born in Britain. But the debate was memorable for the remark of a girl from Birmingham: "I know that I am British by law but I want to feel it!". However, it is true that our black young people feel a lot more British when they travel on the Continent and when they visit the West Indies they are often referred to as "English youngsters".

First congress of black Catholics

A very important event took place in July, 1990 - the first congress of black Catholics in Britain. "Black" in this context was meant as a socio-political category rather than a strictly ethnic one because it was used to encompass people of Indian, Chinese, Mauritian and Vietnamese origin as well as Afro-Caribbeans. Only Catholics who were black in this sense took part as delegates; a considerable number of white people were invited as observers. I was one of those who doubted the wisdom of having an all-black congress. I took the view that racial issues were the concern of the whole Church and therefore white supporters should take part on the same terms as black. At the same time, I was ready to defer to the wishes of those promoting the project. There were some who thought that such a congress would be divisive. I never took this view; indeed, I defended the intentions of the organisers in a letter to *The Tablet* after the question had been raised.

The congress was conceived, planned and executed by the Catholic Association for Racial Justice (CARJ) who appointed Mrs Betty Luckham of Manchester to co-ordinate the preparations. Two hundred delegates representing most dioceses of England and Wales took part and there were nearly one hundred observers who included some guests from other Christian churches. Cardinal Basil Hume helped to launch the proceedings. Members of our Southwark Congress Group, past and present, gave talks, led sessions and helped to produce the end product of the event - "The Charter for Black Catholics". Our choir, "Bridges", led the highly inspirational masses which were a memorable feature of the weekend. The first of them was concelebrated by a number of English bishops, together with a large contingent of Indian bishops who were visiting London at the time.

The congress has to be judged a remarkable success. The Charter roundly affirmed that there could only be one Catholic Church in Britain and that black people claimed a full part within it. Other affirmations were made about education, family life, young people and vocations to the priesthood and the religious life. Racism in all its forms, including the racism that lurked within the Catholic community, had to be exposed and repudiated.

The mood of the delegates was sometimes critical but always loyal. All who took part in the congress or came under its influence through the widespread distribution and discussion of the Charter are likely to have gained a heightened sense of belonging and a fresh sense of reponsibility as Catholics. It must certainly be seen as a milestone in the development of a black participation in the British Catholic community.

The international dimension

In discussing multi-racial development in Britain, we need to be aware that the racial question is an international problem. We have reflected a little on the situation in North America. In early 1992, we can marvel at the progress being made in South Africa - the very home of apartheid. First, we had the release of Nelson Mandela and the extraordinary dignity with which he has lifted the aspirations of black South Africans and conducted negotiations with the white government. And with the statesman-like bearing of Mandela, we also have seen the wisdom and courage of F W de Klerk. Having been astonished by the turn-around of events in the old Soviet Union and Eastern Europe, we now have this revolution in

South Africa to wonder at. It is devoutly to be hoped that this too proves to be a predominantly peaceful revolution. No doubt, historians will argue over the role of international pressure in bringing about change in South Africa - whether the balance of wisdom was on the side of moderate opposition by such as Margaret Thatcher or whether the full-blown sanctions party were in the long run more effective. I favour the attitude of people like Ian Botham. He was never stridently critical of white South Africa; he was simply implacable in his refusal to play cricket with them while apartheid lasted.

In November, 1991 our Congress Group addressed itself to the European dimension of race relations. The consolidation of European economic union in 1992 and the social and political issues due to be settled at the impending Maastricht summit of December, 1991, had created anxieties in our British black community. Few if any Continental countries had anti-discriminatory laws comparable with the British Race Relations Act. Though British black people would have full legal rights of movement, employment and abode throughout the EEC, how would this work out in countries such as Spain or Greece where black people were almost unknown? Indeed, there were even more acute reasons for anxiety in Germany and France where strong semi-Fascist political movements had appeared. Our thoughts at the Congress Group meeting were guided by a black lady professionally engaged in race relations in London and a leader-writer for a national daily newspaper who was a specialist in European affairs. Our discussion made it clear to our journalist guest - a strong pro-European - that too little thought had been given to the interests of our black community in the great European debate. He advised us to represent our anxieties to the Foreign Office and gave us the name of an official to write to. This was duly done on our behalf.

Golden moments

This story of the South London Catholic Caribbean Chaplaincy is nearly told and with it my opinions about the state of race relations in Britain in the early 1990s. But there are two special chaplaincy events still to relate. One of them was sad but proved also to be an inspiration; the other was a celebration which turned out to be a kind of summing up. Both took place at St Anselm's Church, Tooting Bec.

Mention has been made of Marjorie Redhead who came to look after our chaplaincy house in 1978 and whose warmth and devotion was a very important part of the attraction of the house from then on. In April, 1987, after a very short illness, Marjorie died one Sunday morning from heart failure. Our whole community converged on St Anselm's, the nearest large Church to us, for her requiem Mass. We filled the Church, "Bridges" sang a most beautiful Mass which lasted nearly two hours. I celebrated the Mass with our area bishop presiding. Priests from Australia and Trinidad took part and one of our priest friends came specially from Ireland to be with us.

Marjorie's family in Trinidad had asked that her body should be brought home for burial. Accordingly, I travelled with her coffin to Trinidad. We had an equally beautiful farewell in the Catholic Church in Princes' Town - nearly all Marjorie's large family lived in or near there. She was carried into Church by eight young nephews. The Trinidadian parish priest conducted the funeral requiem, a priest friend from my first visit in 1975 also took part and I was the preacher. It seemed as if all Princes' Town was there. After the Mass we laid her to rest just outside the west door alongside her mother and her brother.

Back at John Archer House we determined upon a memorial for her in the garden. We set up a statue of Our Lady, for whom Marjorie had a great devotion, on a specially prepared plinth with an inscription. All around was a rockery which she had spent many hours tending. We had a special Sunday evening Mass to dedicate it. Our friends again came from far and wide, Bridges sang, our area bishop again took great trouble to be with us, and, most delightful of all, Marjorie's brother, sister and sister-in-law came from Trinidad to join us. So Marjorie's departure was a marvellous experience of Christian community embracing London and the West Indies and spanning too earth and heaven .

The other event was my Silver Jubilee celebrations in April, 1991. Again we filled St Anselm's to over-flowing. Our community were the hosts. A lot of my friends from many different scenes were invited, including Anglican friends. Indeed the former Anglican Bishop of Birmingham, an old friend from the time we both worked in Cambridge, paid me the compliment of coming and saying friendly words about me. We had another beautiful Mass which was not short. A large number of priest and deacon friends took part. I was flanked by Deacons Charles Gaillard and Braz Menezes, the latter a Goan friend. The preacher was a friend with whom I shared an enthusiasm for both the YCW and the spirituality of Father Charles de Foucauld and the movement in the Church which he engendered. We were fortunate to have near St Anselm's one of the largest halls in South West London belonging to the Polish Community. Even this was scarcely big enough for the crowd. The efforts of our large organising team were equal to the task of providing enough for everyone to eat and drink, but only just!

This celebration was the culmination of the chaplaincy's first eighteen years. It was a splendid affirmation of all that we had done together. There is no need to extenuate one's failures and inadequacies - these are part of the story and a reminder that the work of God is a lot larger than merely human efforts. But the Silver Jubilee for me was a heart warming message that we had shared many blessings and that we had not been labouring in vain. I remarked during the proceedings that the day would come when the people could well do without me but I was not sure that I could now do without them.